Euthecia Hancewicz

Joan M. Kenney

D0128343

# Literacy Strategies for Improving

# Mathematics Instruction

 Association for Supervision and Curriculum Development • Alexandria, Virginia USA

Association for Supervision and Curriculum Development
1703 N. Beauregard St. • Alexandria, VA 22311-1714 USA
Phone: 800-933-2723 or 703-578-9600 • Fax: 703-575-5400
Web site: www.ascd.org • E-mail: member@ascd.org
Author guidelines: www.ascd.org/write

Gene R. Carter, *Executive Director;* Nancy Modrak, *Director of Publishing;* Julie Houtz, *Director of Book Editing & Production;* Ernesto Yermoli, *Project Manager;* Georgia Park, *Senior Graphic Designer;* BMWW, *Typesetter;* Dina Murray Seamon, *Production Specialist*

All Web links in this book are correct as of the publication date below but may have become inactive or otherwise modified since that time. If you notice a deactivated or changed link, please e-mail books@ascd.org with the words "Link Update" in the subject line. In your message, please specify the Web link, the book title, and the page number on which the link appears.

Paperback ISBN-13: 978-1-4166-0230-9 • Paperback ISBN-10: 1-4166-0230-5
ASCD product #105137     s10/05

Also available as an e-book through ebrary, netLibrary, and many online book sellers (see Books in Print for the ISBNs).

Quantity discounts for the paperback book: 10–49 copies, 10%; 50+ copies, 15%; for 500 or more copies, call 800-933-2723, ext. 5634, or 703-575-5634.

**Library of Congress Cataloging-in-Publication Data**

Literacy strategies for improving mathematics instruction / Joan M. Kenney . . . [et al.].
    p.  cm.
    Includes bibliographical references and index.
    ISBN 1-4166-0230-5 (pbk. : alk. paper)   1. Mathematics—Study and teaching.
I. Kenney, Joan M., 1937–  II. Association for Supervision and Curriculum Development.

    QA11.2.L58   2005
    510'.71—dc22                                                    2005016434

# Literacy Strategies for Improving
# Mathematics Instruction

# Preface

*School days, school days,*
*Dear old Golden Rule days.*
*Reading and 'Riting and 'Rithmetic,*
*Taught to the tune of a hick-ry stick . . .*

At the time this song was popular, the mark of an educated person was basic facility in each of the disciplines of reading, writing, and mathematics. These were viewed as discrete topics and taught in relative isolation of each other, although effective writing was seen as a somewhat logical result of skill in reading. The notion that mathematics textbooks were to be read for content, or that mathematics problems were to be solved by producing anything other than a numerical answer, was totally foreign. Indeed, reading and writing in mathematics did not become a subject of serious discussion and research until the appearance of the standards-based mathematics curricula of the 1990s, driven by the National Council of Teachers of Mathematics (NCTM) standards of 1991. Suddenly a clearer distinction between arithmetic and mathematics was put forward. The ability to master and demonstrate mathematical knowledge came to be seen as the result of a process that involves teaching for understanding, student-centered learning, concept-building rather than memorization of facts, and the ability to communicate mathematical understanding to others.

This book blends current research on selected aspects of language literacy with practitioner evidence of the unique challenges presented in transferring these language skills to the mathematics classroom. It is distinctive in that it not only looks extensively at current literacy research, but also connects the research to actual practice and the development of concrete classroom strategies. We present the etymological underpinnings for thinking about mathematics as a language, and describe the unique difficulties encountered in reading mathematics text and creating a mathematics vocabulary. We also look at the new role of mathematics teacher as reading teacher, and differentiate between what literacy looks like in the language arts classroom and in the mathematics classroom. Most importantly, however, this book is designed to provide educators with a broad spectrum of tools to use as they work to transform students into confident communicators and practitioners of mathematics.

Joan M. Kenney
*Balanced Assessment Program*

Euthecia Hancewicz
Diana Metsisto
Loretta Heuer
Cynthia L. Tuttle
*Massachusetts Mathematics Coaching Project*

# 1

# Mathematics as Language

*Joan M. Kenney*

Over the years, we have colloquially referred to mathematics as a special language. Yet practitioners have had little research to consult on the matter, or impetus to reflect on whether the process of learning the language of mathematics is similar to that of learning any other second language.

Although researchers have paid lip service to the unique vocabulary of mathematics, they have done little to highlight the ambiguities, double meanings, and other "word" problems associated with the discipline. Ignorance of these issues can lead to impaired communication at best, and serious mathematical misunderstanding at worst. To compound the difficulty, information in mathematics texts is presented in a bewildering assortment of ways; in attempting to engage students, textbook writers too often introduce graphic distraction, and format the pages in ways that obscure the basic concepts. In this book we look carefully and reflectively at the difficulties inherent in learning the language of mathematics, and suggest strategies for how best to overcome them.

There are over 4,000 languages and dialects in the world, and all of them share one thing in common: they have a category for words representing nouns, or objects, and a category for words representing verbs, or actions. Taking this commonality as a starting point provides an interesting way of looking at the mathematical world and its language. It is possible to identify both content and process dimensions in mathematics, but unlike many disciplines, in which *process* refers to general reasoning and logic skills, in mathematics the term refers to skills that are domain-specific. As a result, people tend to lump content and process together when discussing mathematics, calling it all mathematics *content*. However, it is vitally important to maintain a distinction between mathematical content and process, because the distinction reflects something very significant about the way humans approach mental activity of any sort. All human languages have grammatical structures that distinguish between nouns and verbs; these structures express the distinction between the objects themselves and the actions carried out by or on the objects.

A model first proposed by the Balanced Assessment Program at the Harvard Graduate School of Education (Schwartz & Kenney, 1995) suggests that we think about mathematical nouns, or objects, as being numbers, measurements, shapes, spaces, functions, patterns, data, and arrangements—items that comfortably map onto commonly accepted mathematics content strands. Mathematical verbs may be regarded as the four predominant actions that we ascribe to problem-solving and reasoning:

- *Modeling and formulating.* Creating appropriate representations and relationships to mathematize the original problem.
- *Transforming and manipulating.* Changing the mathematical form in which a problem is originally expressed to equivalent forms that represent solutions.
- *Inferring.* Applying derived results to the original problem situation, and interpreting and generalizing the results in that light.
- *Communicating.* Reporting what has been learned about a problem to a specified audience.

Taken as a whole, these four actions represent the process that we go through to solve a problem. Taken individually, they represent actions that students can develop and on which they can be assessed. To view the actions individually also enables us to separate the type of proficiency required in, for instance, manipulation and transformation, which are primarily skill-based actions, from the more complex proficiencies required to create a mathematical model and to generalize and extend the results of a mathematical action. Also, because not all exercises make equal demands on or involve equivalent competency in each of the mathematical objects and actions, students will not necessarily perform evenly across them. For example, the ability of learners to model a problem involving functions may be quite different from their ability to model a problem involving data. Students may vary in their abilities to communicate their understanding of geometric objects, and objects of number and quantity. Here again, it is important to keep the distinction between mathematical objects and actions explicit while viewing student work; otherwise, comprehensive assessment of student mathematical understanding will be severely limited.

According to Schwartz (1996), dividing the elements of mathematics into objects and actions has significant implications for curriculum:

> To a large extent the arithmetic curriculum of the elementary school as well as the algebra curriculum of the middle and high school focus on the manipulation of symbols *representing* mathematical objects, rather than on *using* mathematical objects in the building and analyzing of arithmetic or algebraic models. Thus, in the primary levels, most of the mathematical time and attention of both teachers and students is devoted to the teaching and learning of the computational algorithms for the addition, subtraction, multiplication, and division of integers and decimal and non-decimal fractions. Later, the teaching and learning of algebra becomes, in large measure, the teaching and learning of the algebraic notational system and its formal, symbolic manipulation. Using the mathematical objects and actions as the basis for modeling one's surround is a neglected piece of the mathematics education enterprise. (p. 39)

But before we can use mathematical objects to model our surround, we must first acquire them. For many reasons, this is an extremely difficult process. Mathematics truly is a foreign language for most students: it is learned almost entirely at school and is not spoken at home. Mathematics is not a "first" language; that is, it does not originate as a spoken language, except for the naming of small whole numbers. Mathematics has both formal and informal expressions, which we might characterize as "school math" and "street math" (Usiskin, 1996). When we attempt to engage students by using real-world examples, we often find that the colloquial or "street" language does not always map directly or correctly onto the mathematical syntax. For example, suppose a pre-algebra student is asked to symbolically express that there are twice as many dogs as cats in the local animal shelter. The equation $2C=D$ describes the distribution, but is it true that two cats are equivalent to one dog?

Recasting the mathematics domain into objects and actions can also help to illuminate the similarities and differences between how we learn the language of mathematics and how we learn any other second language. My coauthors and I were all viewed as "good in math"—that is, fluent in the mathematics language. As we compared our earliest memories of learning mathematics, one of us remembered being made aware of numbers as an abstract quantity by looking at the pattern of classroom windowpanes. Another, who characterizes herself as a very visual learner, recalled seeing boxes of six pansies apiece packed in cartons of four boxes apiece at her family's floral business—an observation that triggered previously undiscovered ideas about addition and multiplication. Another member of the group, whose father was a banker, remembered dinner-table conversations filled with mental mathematics problems, yet she tends to rely heavily on writing as a learning tool. And one of us told of feeling suddenly "divorced" from the language of mathematics upon entering Algebra II, where everything became symbol-laden and obscure.

Despite our varying introductions to and degrees of comfort with mathematical language, my coauthors and I have retained knowledge of the language of mathematics far better than knowledge of the spoken languages we studied. Even though most of us took two or three years of a foreign language in high school, we have not been able to sustain our use of it in any expansive way. Certainly some of this can be explained by our lack of daily use of the languages, but another factor may be at work—namely, the *way* we learned them, mainly by memorizing vocabulary words and verb conjugations out of any immediate context. Is this not similar to the way students may successfully memorize number facts and plug into algorithms when learning arithmetic? However, when these students are later asked to draw inferences, discriminate between quantities, or justify solutions, the full effect of their lack of mathematics fluency becomes apparent.

Another interesting commonality between mathematics and foreign languages lies in the relationship between rhyme and retention. Several in our group either did not initially speak English as a first language, or were essentially bilingual for a period of time in both a "home" language and a "school" language. What we tend to retain of the second language is most easily accessed through music or rhyme—we remember songs, prayers, and poems even though we can no longer perform even the most rudimentary task of written or spoken communication. This brings to mind students who are able to spout mathematical facts using jingles or mnemonics, but cannot use the facts in any extended way or for any new purpose.

Perhaps the greatest difficulty in learning the language of mathematics is that a double decoding must go on during the entire process. Particularly in the early stages, we must decode spoken mathematics words in the initial context of normal parlance, and then translate to the different context of mathematics usage. Double decoding also occurs when we first encounter written mathematics words or symbols, which must first be decoded, and then connected to a concept that may or may not be present in prior knowledge even in an elementary way.

As developmentally complex as double decoding is for most students, imagine how difficult it must be for second-language learners. The following anecdote illustrates the problem.

As I observed a 4th grade classroom, the teacher began by discussing whole numbers; she then moved to the distinction between even and odd numbers. When asked to classify numbers as even or odd, one of the students, a recent Hispanic immigrant with limited English skills, consistently marked the numbers 6 and 10 as odd. When asked to explain, he said, "Those whole numbers are not multiples of 2." Additional conversation between teacher and student did little to clarify the problem until I asked the student what he meant by "whole numbers." It was only when he answered "6, 8, 9, 10, and maybe 3" that we realized that this student had constructed a mental model of "hole" numbers—that is, numbers formed by sticks and holes—and that this was, to him, a totally consistent explanation. If a number had only one "hole," like the numbers 6, 9, and 10, it was odd, because the number of "holes" was not a multiple of 2. The number 3 was problematic in this student's system, because he couldn't decide whether it was really two holes if you completed the image, or two half-holes that could be combined to make a single one. Though this anecdote may seem bizarre, it richly illustrates the difficulty students have as they struggle to make meaning of the words they hear in the mathematics classroom.

Another difficulty inherent in the decoding process stems from the fact that, although most mathematical nouns actually describe the things they refer to, their origins are usually Latin or Greek rather than English. The work of Steven Schwartzman (1994) has traced these connections. The mathematics words that we use in English come from many sources, and have assumed their current forms as a result of various processes; in addition, many contain more than one unit of meaning. Even though English, Greek, and Latin are all rooted in the Indo-European language—the common ancestor of the languages spoken by roughly half of the people in the world today—few American students currently have any exposure to either Greek or Latin.

An interesting example of how language can either illuminate or obscure concepts is the difference between the word "twelve" in English and the corresponding word in Chinese, the grammar of which is a perfect reflection of decimal structure. One day, as I was observing the piloting of a manipulative device designed to help students understand place value, I talked at length with a Chinese-born teacher who was using the device in his classroom. He told me that in his native language there are only nine names for the numbers 1 through 9, and three multipliers (10, 100, and 1,000). In order to name a number, you read its decomposition in base 10, so that 12 means "ten and two." This elegant formalism contrasts sharply with the 29 words needed to express the same numbers in English, where, in addition to the words for the numbers 1 through 9, there are special words for the numbers 11 through 19 and the decades from 20 to 90, none of which can be predicted from the words for the other numerals. To compound the confusion, the English word for 12 incorporates two units of meaning: The first part of the word comes from Latin and Greek expressions for "two," and the second part is related to an Indo-European root meaning "leave" (Wylde & Partridge, 1963). Thus, an etymological decoding would be "the number that leaves 2 behind when 10, the base in which we do our calculating, is subtracted from it"—far from transparent to the novice learner!

It is also important to recognize the potential for enormous confusion that symbolic representations can create. As Barton and Heidema (2002) note:

> In reading mathematics text one must decode and comprehend not only words, but also signs and symbols, which involve different skills. Decoding words entails connecting sounds to the alphabetic symbols, or letters. . . . In contrast, mathematics signs and symbols may be pictorial, or they may refer to an operation, or to an expression. Consequently, students need to learn the meaning of each symbol much like they learn "sight" words in the English language. In addition they need to connect each symbol, the idea it represents, and the written or spoken term that corresponds to the idea. (p. 15)

The confounding potential of symbolic representation cannot be overstated. Younger students can be quite mystified by the fact that changing the orientation of a symbol—for example, from horizontal (=) to vertical (||)—can completely change its meaning. Figure 1.1 is a collection of confusing words, symbols, and formats that we have encountered in the classroom. This is not an exhaustive list; rather, it is intended as a work-in-progress that teachers are encouraged to add to, and as an early-warning system for educators who are mystified by the misinterpretations particular students may attribute to a mathematical situation that, to others, has quite a different meaning.

| FIGURE 1.1 | Confusing Terms, Formats, and Symbols in Mathematics |
|---|---|

**CONFUSING TERMS**

| | | |
|---|---|---|
| altitude | imaginary | radical |
| any | limit | range |
| base | mean and median | reflection |
| combination | multiples | regular |
| compute and computer | number and numeral | relationship |
| congruent and equivalent | of and off | remainder (division) vs. |
| difference | operation |    remainder (subtraction) |
| divide *by* and divide *into* | or (exclusive) vs. or | right angle and left angle |
| dividend |   (inclusive) | similar |
| equal and equivalent | origin | sine and sign |
| example | pi | sum and some |
| extreme | power | tangent |
| factor | prime | variable |
| fact | product | |

**CONFUSING FORMATS**

analog and digital clocks
angle rotation
quadrant layout
superscripts and subscripts
various types of graphs

**CONFUSING SYMBOLS**

$\sqrt{\phantom{x}}$ and $\overline{)\phantom{x}}$

$\bullet$ , $\times$ , $(\phantom{x})$ , and $*$

$\div$ , $\overline{)\phantom{x}}$ , $/$ , and $\frac{m}{n}$

$=$ , $\equiv$ , $\sim$ , $\approx$ , and $\cong$

$<$ and $>$

To summarize, in mathematics, *vocabulary* may be confusing because the words mean different things in mathematics and nonmathematics contexts, because two different words sound the same, or because more than one word is used to describe the same concept. *Symbols* may be confusing either because they look alike (e.g., the division and square root symbols) or because different representations may be used to describe the same process (e.g., •, *, and × for multiplication). *Graphic representations* may be confusing because of formatting variations (e.g., bar graphs versus line graphs) or because the graphics are not consistently read in the same direction.

Throughout this book, we will explore how mathematics instruction can be made deeper and more stimulating through skill-building in reading and writing. We will also discuss the importance of graphic representations and classroom discourse. As Barnett-Clarke and Ramirez (2004) note: "As teachers, we must learn to carefully choose the language pathways that support mathematical understanding, and simultaneously, we must be alert for language pitfalls that contribute to misunderstandings of mathematical ideas. More specifically, we must learn how to invite, support, and model thoughtful explanation, evaluation, and revision of mathematical ideas using correct mathematical terms and symbols" (p. 56).

The intent of this book is to facilitate this invitation, this support, and this modeling by opening classroom doors and sharing the wisdom of teachers who have reflected deeply on how best to create and extend the mathematical fluency of their students.

# 2

# Reading in the Mathematics Classroom

*Diana Metsisto*

*The students know how to do the math, they just don't understand what the question is asking.*

*The thing I don't like about this new series is the way the problems are stated; they're hard for the students to get what to do.*

*The reading level is too hard for the students.*

*I have to simplify, to reword the questions for my students, and then they can do it.*

In my three years working as a mathematics coach to 6th, 7th, and 8th grade teachers, I've often heard statements such as these. There seems to be an idea that somehow it is unfair to expect students to interpret problems on standardized tests and in curriculum texts: after all, what does evaluating student reading skills have to do with mathematics? When people I meet find out that I teach mathematics, they often say, "I did OK in math—except for those word problems."

To many teachers, mathematics is simply a matter of cueing up procedures for students, who then perform the appropriate calculations. Over and over, I hear teachers interpret problems for their students when asked what a question means or when a student says, "I don't know what to do." This started me thinking about the mathematics teacher's role in helping students to interpret problems.

Certainly teachers try to help students to read and interpret mathematics text and discuss problem-solving strategies with them. I hear them say such things as "*of* means *times*" and "*total* means you probably have to add something." However, when you think about it, most strategies are still procedural—"follow

9

this recipe"—rather than about helping students to read for understanding (i.e., to interpret text and to reason).

Unless mathematics teachers are generalists and have been trained in reading instruction, they don't see literacy as part of their skill set. More important, they don't appreciate that reading a mathematics text or problem is really very different from other types of reading, requiring specific strategies unique to mathematics. In addition, most reading teachers do not teach the skills necessary to successfully read in mathematics class.

Listening to teachers reword or interpret mathematics problems for their students has led me to start conversations with teachers about taking time to work specifically on reading and interpretation. One strategy we arrived at is for teachers to model their thinking out loud as they read and figure out what a problem is asking them to do. Other strategies include dialoguing with students about any difficulties they may have in understanding a problem and asking different students to share their understanding. The strategies that we have shared have come from years of working in the classroom to improve student comprehension. None of us had previously studied the unique difficulties involved in reading mathematics texts.

All mathematics teachers recognize the need to teach their students to read and interpret what I'll call mathematical sentences: equations and inequalities. The National Council of Teachers of Mathematics (1996) states that, "[b]ecause mathematics is so often conveyed in symbols, oral and written communication about mathematical ideas is not always recognized as an important part of mathematics education. Students do not necessarily talk about mathematics naturally; teachers need to help them to do so" (p. 60). Knowing how to use the unique symbols that make up the shorthand of mathematical statements—such as numerals, operation signs, and variables that stand in for numbers—has always been part of what mathematics teachers are expected to teach. So in a limited way, we have always been reading teachers without realizing it.

Martinez and Martinez (2001) highlight the importance of reading to mathematics students:

> [Students] . . . learn to use language to focus and work through problems, to communicate ideas coherently and clearly, to organize ideas and structure arguments, to extend their thinking and knowledge to encompass other perspectives and experiences, to understand their own problem-solving and thinking processes as well as those of others, and to develop

flexibility in representing and interpreting ideas. At the same time, they begin to see mathematics, not as an isolated school subject, but as a life subject—an integral part of the greater world, with connections to concepts and knowledge encountered across the curriculum. (p. 47)

James Bullock (1994) defines mathematics as a form of language invented by humans to discuss abstract concepts of numbers and space. He states that the power of the language is that it enables scientists to construct metaphors, which scientists call "models." Mathematical models enable us to think critically about physical phenomena and explore in depth their underlying ideas. Our traditional form of mathematics education is really training, not education, and has deprived our students of becoming truly literate. Knowing what procedures to perform on cue, as a trained animal performs tricks, is not the basic purpose of learning mathematics. Unless we can apply mathematics to real life, we have not learned the discipline.

If we intend for students to understand mathematical concepts rather than to produce specific performances, we must teach them to engage meaningfully with mathematics texts. When we talk about students learning to read such texts, we refer to a transaction in which the reader is able to ponder the ideas that the text presents. The meaning that readers draw will depend largely on their prior knowledge of the information and on the kinds of thinking they do after they read the text (Draper, 2002): Can they synthesize the information? Can they decide what information is important? Can they draw inferences from what they've read?

## Reading Requirements for Mathematics Text

Let's look at some ways in which mathematics text differs from text in other subjects. Research has shown that mathematics texts contain more concepts per sentence and paragraph than any other type of text. They are written in a very compact style; each sentence contains a lot of information, with little redundancy. The text can contain words as well as numeric and non-numeric symbols to decode. In addition, a page may be laid out in such a way that the eye must travel in a different pattern than the traditional left-to-right one of most reading. There may also be graphics that must be understood for the text to make sense; these may sometimes include information that is intended to add to the comprehension of a problem but instead may be distracting.

Finally, many texts are written above the grade level for which they are intended (Barton & Heidema, 2002).

Most mathematics textbooks include a variety of sidebars containing prose and pictures both related and unrelated to the main topic being covered. In these we might find a mixed review of previous work, extra skills practice, a little vignette from an almanac, a historical fact, or a connection to something from another culture. Such sidebars often contain a series of questions that are not part of the actual exercises. Although they are probably added to give color and interest to the look of the page, they can be very confusing to readers, who might wonder what they are supposed to be paying attention to. Spending time early in the year analyzing the structure of the mathematics textbook with students can help them to read and comprehend that text.

When I reflect on my own experiences in the classroom, I realize that students need help finding their way around a new text. They often will just read one sentence after another, not differentiating among problem statements, explanatory information, and supportive prose. As we strive to develop independent learners, asking students questions about the text structure can help them to focus on the idea that texts have an underlying organization, that different texts may have different structures, and that it is important to analyze the structure of the text being used.

In addition to the unique page formatting and structure of most mathematics texts, the basic structure of mathematics problems differs from that of most informational writing. In a traditional reading paragraph, there is a topic sentence at the beginning and the remaining sentences fill in details that expand on and support this main idea; in a mathematics problem, the key idea often comes at the end of the paragraph, in the form of a question or statement to find something (e.g., "How many apples are left?" "Find the area and perimeter of the figure above."). Students must learn to read through the problem to ascertain the main idea and then read it again to figure out which details and numbers relate to the question being posed and which are redundant. Students have to visualize the problem's context and then apply strategies that they think will lead to a solution, using the appropriate data from the problem statement.

Some of the symbols, words, notations, and formats in which numbers appear can be confusing. For instance, when do you use the word *number* as opposed to *numeral*? Do you indicate numbers with numeric symbols, or with words? The term *remainder* can be used in problems solved by both division and subtraction. The equal sign can represent quantities of exactly the same value, or items that are equivalent.

I have seen students read 12:10 on a digital clock and interpret it as meaning 12⁄10 hours instead of 12⅙. This illustrates the difficulty of using digital clocks to help students picture elapsed time: digital clocks only present us with digits for isolated moments in time, whereas analog clocks—with their circular faces, hand angles, and pie wedges—provide a concrete model of the fractional parts of an hour, thus adding to our understanding of how time is divided.

## Same Words, Different Languages

Adding to the confusion of this dense language of symbols is the fact that many mathematical terms have different meanings in everyday use. For example, the word *similar* means "alike" in everyday usage, whereas in mathematics it means that the ratios of the corresponding sides of two shapes are equivalent and corresponding angles are equal. Thus in everyday English, all rectangles are "similar" because they are alike, whereas in mathematics they are "similar" only if the ratio of the short sides equals the ratio of the long sides. Mathematical terms such as *prime, median, mean, mode, product, combine, dividend, height, difference, example,* and *operation* all have different meanings in common parlance.

In addition to words, mathematical statements and questions are also understood differently when made in a non-mathematical context. For example, right angles are often drawn with one vertical line and with one perpendicular line extending from it to the right. When shown a right angle with the perpendicular line extending to the left, a student once asked a colleague of mine, "Is that a left angle?"

According to Reuben Hersh (1997), students must be taught that the language we read and speak in mathematics class is actually a technical jargon, even though it may look and sound like regular English. For example, zero is not really a number in everyday language—when we say we have "a number of books" in English, we never mean zero (or one, for that matter). But in mathematics, 0 and 1 are both acceptable answers denoting the concept of "a number." Similarly, when we "add" something in English, we invariably mean that we are increasing something. In mathematics, however, addition can result in an increase, a decrease, or no change at all depending on what number is being added. Hersh adds the following example: The answer to the question, "If you subtract zero from zero, what's the difference?" is, in mathematics, zero. We are explicitly asking for a numerical answer. But in English, the question can be interpreted as, "Who cares?" (i.e., "What's the difference?").

When a girl in a class I was observing was asked, in reference to a city map, "How might you go from City Hall to the police station?" she replied, "By car, walk—I don't know." She understood "how" to mean "by what means" rather than "by following what path." This student is not alone in finding such mathematics questions puzzling.

## Small Words, Big Differences

In English there are many small words, such as pronouns, prepositions, and conjunctions, that make a big difference in student understanding of mathematics problems. For example:

• The words *of* and *off* cause a lot of confusion in solving percentage problems, as the percent *of* something is quite distinct from the percent *off* something.

• The word *a* can mean "any" in mathematics. When asking students to "show that a number divisible by 6 is even," we aren't asking for a specific example, but for the students to show that all numbers divisible by 6 have to be even.

• When we take the area "of" a triangle, we mean what the students think of as "inside" the triangle.

• The square (second power) "of" the hypotenuse gives the same numerical value as the area of the square that can be constructed "on" the hypotenuse.

A study by Kathryn Sullivan (1982) showed that even a brief, three-week program centered on helping students distinguish the mathematical usage of "small" words can significantly improve student mathematics computation scores. Words studied in the program cited by Sullivan include *the, is, a, are, can, on, who, find, one, ones, ten, tens, and, or, number, numeral, how, many, how many, what, write, it, each, which, do, all, same, exercises, here, there, has,* and *have.*

I remember once observing a lesson on multiplying fractions using an area model. The teacher had asked me to script her "launch"—the segment of the lesson designed to prepare students for a paired or small-group exploration of the topic. Because the teacher felt that the mathematics textbook was too difficult for her students, she read the text aloud and asked students to restate what she said in their own words. My notes show that the teacher spoke in a soft, conversational tone. She clearly enunciated the content vocabulary required for the lesson and clarified the meanings of nouns and adjectives related to the topic, and of the verbs for the procedures necessary to complete the activity. However, my notes also showed that some pronouns had ambiguous referents (e.g., "You multiply *it* . . .") and that the teacher's soft tone made some prepositions barely audible. For example, the text asked students to find half of 2¼ pans of brownies (the teacher read it as "two and a fourth"). If they weren't following along in their books, what did the students hear—"two *'nda* fourth" or "two *'nta* fourths"? As a matter of fact, one student took a sheet of notebook paper and wrote "2/4" at the top. Next, he drew two squares. Finally he used horizontal lines to divide each square into fourths. I pointed to the "2/4" and asked what it meant. He replied, "Two-fourths is two pans divided *into* fourths." And to that particular student, half of *that* quantity was one.

Enunciating small but significant words more precisely, being more aware of the confusion that these words can engender, and emphasizing the correct use of these little land mines will not only enhance computational skills, but also help students answer open-response questions more accurately.

## Strategic Reading

Literacy researchers have developed some basic strategies for reading to learn. Here is a summary of strategies outlined by Draper (2002):

Before reading, the strategic reader
- Previews the text by looking at the title, the pictures, and the print in order to evoke relevant thoughts and memories
- Builds background by activating appropriate prior knowledge about what he or she already knows about the topic (or story), the vocabulary, and the form in which the topic (or story) is presented
- Sets purposes for reading by asking questions about what he or she wants to learn (know) during the reading episode

While reading, the strategic reader
- Checks understanding of the text by paraphrasing the author's words

- Monitors comprehension by using context clues to figure out unknown words and by imagining, inferencing, and predicting
- Integrates new concepts with existing knowledge, continually revising purposes for reading

After reading, the strategic reader
- Summarizes what has been read by retelling the plot of the story or the main idea of the text
- Evaluates the ideas contained in the text
- Makes applications of the ideas in the text to unique situations, extending the ideas to broader perspectives. (p. 524)

Mathematics teachers can use this general outline in several ways. They can model the process by reading the problem out loud and paraphrasing the author's words and then talking through how they use context clues to figure out word meanings. Before reading, teachers can ask questions that they want students to consider as they approach a mathematics problem. Teachers can probe about the reading's vocabulary by asking questions such as, "Are we clear on the meaning of all of the words?" or "Does the context help or should we look the word up?" Also significant are questions about the meaning of the problem, such as, "Can I paraphrase the problem?" "Does the problem make sense to me?" or "Does my understanding incorporate everything I've read?"

Reinforcing the idea that a piece of mathematics text *needs* to make sense (and that it *can* make sense) is exceedingly important. Teachers need to provide explicit scaffolding experiences to help students connect the text to their prior knowledge and to build such knowledge. In her book *Yellow Brick Roads* (2003), Janet Allen suggests that teachers need to ask themselves the following critical questions about a text:
- What is the major concept?
- How can I help students connect this concept to their lives?
- Are there key concepts or specialized vocabulary that needs to be introduced because students could not get meaning from the context?
- How could we use the pictures, charts, and graphs to predict or anticipate content?
- What supplemental materials do I need to provide to support reading?

Consider the following three situations I encountered while working with two 6th grade mathematics teachers and an 8th grade mathematics teacher:

• In the first case, the 6th grade teacher was explicitly teaching students how to look for context clues. The question at hand required students to write "$7 \times 7 \times 7 \times 8 \times 9 \times 9$" in exponential notation. The teacher suggested that the students look for a word in the text of the question that might help them. It was interesting to see the different ways that students interpreted this simple exercise. Some seemingly did not look at the words at all; they simply executed the calculation. Some knew the word *notation* and knew that *write* meant to reformat the problem. Those who also knew the word *exponent* were able to answer the problem correctly, whereas some of those who didn't know what *exponent* meant used a different type of notation to rewrite the problem in words. It is clear that simple exercises such as these can help students to interpret mathematics text by looking at *all* the words, rather than assuming that a calculation is always sought.

• In the second case, students in a 6th grade class were asked to find the percentage of cat owners who said their cats had bad breath. In a survey, 80 out of 200 cat owners had said yes. The students used several different strategies to answer the question and discussed it as a class. They were then asked to read and answer some follow-up questions. The first one read, "If you survey 500 cat owners, about how many would you expect to say that their cats have bad breath? Explain your reasoning." The students asked the teacher to help them understand what was being asked, and she complied, as teachers often do without thinking, by telling the students to use the 40 percent figure from the previous question.

If we are really trying to help students read and understand for themselves, we must ask them questions instead of explicitly telling them what the text means: "What information do you have that might help you answer this question?" "Does the fact that this is a 'follow-up' help us to decipher the question?"

• In the third case, groups of 8th graders worked through a series of problems involving compound interest calculations. The main question read, "What are the initial value, rate of increase in value, and number of years that Sam is assuming?" In one group, a boy said loudly, "It's too hard to figure out! I don't want to use my brain," and snapped his book shut. When questioned about his reaction, the boy just said, "Too many questions."

Students often have difficulty with this sort of multipart question. They need to develop the simple strategy of taking the main question apart and listing the individual questions separately.

As a teacher, I often had students come to me for help understanding a problem. Just asking them to read the problem aloud would usually elicit, "Oh, now I get it." My experience suggests that having students read problems aloud to themselves can help their understanding. I also think that, for some students, the attention of someone else listening may help them to focus.

## Other Reading Strategies

In addition to helping students learn the meaning in mathematics text of "little" mathematics words and the precise mathematical meanings of familiar English words, teachers should help them understand the abstract, unfamiliar terminology of mathematics. As stated by Barton, Heidema, and Jordan (2002), and as I've learned from my own experience in the classroom, just giving students vocabulary lists with definitions, or asking them to look up the definitions, isn't enough for them to develop the conceptual meaning behind the words or to read and use the vocabulary accurately.

Teachers can also introduce various maps, webs, and other graphic organizers to help students further organize mathematics meanings and concepts. Two graphic organizers that can be particularly useful in mathematics classes are the Frayer Model (Frayer, 1969) and the Semantic Feature Analysis Grid (Baldwin, 1981). In the Frayer Model, a sheet of paper is divided into four quadrants. In the first quadrant, the students define a given term in their own words; in the second quadrant, they list any facts that they know about the word; in the third quadrant, they list examples of the given term; and in the fourth quadrant, they list nonexamples. (See Figure 2.1 for an example of the Frayer Model.)

The Semantic Feature Analysis Grid helps students compare features of mathematical objects that are in the same category by providing a visual prompt of their similarities and differences. On the left side of the grid is a list of terms in the chosen category, and across the top is a list of properties that the objects might share. (An example of the Semantic Feature Analysis Grid is shown in Figure 2.2.)

Another useful problem-solving process is the SQRQCQ process, developed by Leslie Fay (1965), which is a variation of Polya's four-step process (1973). The acronym SQRQCQ stands for the following terms and respective actions:
- *Survey.* Read the problem quickly to get a general understanding of it.
- *Question.* Ask what information the problem requires.

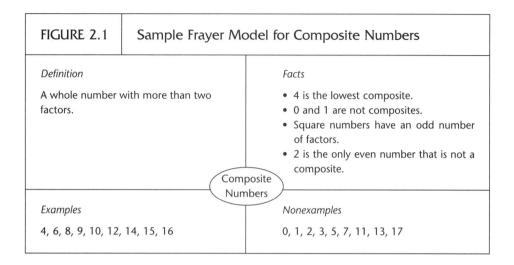

| FIGURE 2.1 | Sample Frayer Model for Composite Numbers |

*Definition*

A whole number with more than two factors.

*Facts*

- 4 is the lowest composite.
- 0 and 1 are not composites.
- Square numbers have an odd number of factors.
- 2 is the only even number that is not a composite.

Composite Numbers

*Examples*

4, 6, 8, 9, 10, 12, 14, 15, 16

*Nonexamples*

0, 1, 2, 3, 5, 7, 11, 13, 17

| FIGURE 2.2 | Sample Semantic Feature Analysis Grid for Quadrilaterals |

| Term | Sides Equal | Angles Equal | Opposite Sides Parallel | Opposite Sides Equal | Only One Pair of Parallel Sides | Four Sides |
|---|---|---|---|---|---|---|
| Parallelogram | | | X | X | | X |
| Rectangle | | X | X | X | | X |
| Rhombus | X | | X | X | | X |
| Scalene Quadrilateral | | | | | | X |
| Square | X | X | X | X | | X |
| Trapezoid | | | | | X | X |

- *Read.* Reread the problem to identify relevant information, facts, and details needed to solve it.
- *Question.* Ask what operations must be performed, and in what order, to solve the problem.
- *Compute/Construct.* Do the computations, or construct the solution.
- *Question.* Ask whether the solution process seems correct and the answer reasonable.

Teachers can model the steps for the students with a chosen problem and then have the students practice individually or in pairs. Students can then be asked to share their use of the strategy with a partner, within a group, or with the class.

# Elementary Classroom Issues

Most elementary teachers teach mathematics as one of several subjects; in many cases, they teach reading as well as mathematics, unlike teachers in middle school and high school. They need to be aware of the particular difficulties involved in reading mathematical text. When encountering mathematical symbols, students face a multilevel decoding process: First they must recognize and separate out the confusing mathematical symbols (e.g., +, ×, <) without any phonic cues; then they must translate each symbol into English; and finally they must connect the symbol to the concept for which it stands and then carry out the operations indicated.

## Graphs and Tables

Graphs are also particularly hard for elementary students to read. The first type of graph that most students encounter is the bar graph, which is most commonly "read" from bottom to top. There are many types of graphs—particularly in the mathematics, science, and social studies contexts—with different "directions of readability."

I became aware of the need to help students learn to stop and analyze graph and table structures when working with (what I thought were) simple matrix puzzles, involving only two rows and two columns, with an operation sign in the upper left corner. The numbers at the top and to the left were to be combined using the operation sign, and the answers were to be written in the interstices of the rows and columns. The idea was for the student to fill in any missing cells in the matrix. (Figure 2.3 is an example of a completed puzzle.)

Several students had difficulty understanding what they were expected to do with the puzzle: What was to be added? Where did the answer go? This experience pointed out to me that specific strategies to decipher graphic representations need to be extensively modeled and repeatedly explored. It is important that students become aware that an underlying plan or pattern can usually be discovered by careful study.

| FIGURE 2.3 | Sample Matrix Puzzle |
|------------|----------------------|

| + | 2 | 6 |
|---|----|----|
| 3 | 5 | 9 |
| 9 | 11 | 15 |

## Guided Reading

One strategy that may be familiar to elementary reading teachers, and which seems particularly useful in the context of mathematics, is that of guided reading sessions (Allen, 2003). In such sessions, the teacher is still responsible for helping students connect what they are reading to prior knowledge. The teacher should first present the text or graphic to students in small, coherent segments, being sure to process each segment before going on to the next one. As the reading progresses, the teacher should ask process questions that she wants the students to ask themselves in the future. They may be asked to predict what the reading will be about simply by reading the title of the piece (if there is one, such as a graph or story problem). Next the students should make two columns on a piece of paper, one headed "What I Predict" and the other headed "What I Know." Once the students have silently read each section of the piece, they should fill out each column accordingly. At this point, the teacher should ask students questions such as the following:

- What would you be doing in that situation?
- Does this make sense?
- What does the picture/graph/chart tell you?
- How does the title connect to what we're reading?
- Why are these words in capital letters?
- Why is there extra white space here?
- What does that word mean in this context?

Figure 2.4 shows a simple example of a possible guided reading for a lesson from an algebra text. The text would be unveiled one paragraph (or equation) at a time rather than given to the students as one continuous passage.

| FIGURE 2.4 | Guided Reading Example |
|---|---|

| TEXT | POSSIBLE QUESTIONS |
|---|---|
| **Solving Systems Using Substitution** | 1. What does the title tell you? |
| *Problem* | |
| From a car wash, a service club made $109 that was divided between the Girl Scouts and the Boy Scouts. There were twice as many girls as boys, so the decision was made to give the girls twice as much money. How much did each group receive? | 2. Before you read further, how would you translate this story problem into equations? |
| *Solution* | |
| Translate each condition into an equation. Suppose the Boy Scouts receive B dollars and the Girl Scouts receive G dollars. We number the equations in the system for reference. | 3. What do they mean here by "condition"? |
| The sum of the amounts is $109. <br> (1) B + G = 109 <br> Girls get twice as much as boys. <br> (2) G = 2B | 4. Did you come up with two equations in answer to question 2 above? Are the equations here the same as yours? If not, how are they different? Can you see a way to substitute? |
| Since G = 2B in equation (2), you can substitute 2B for G in equation (1). | |
| B + 2B = 109 <br> 3B = 109 <br> B = 36 1/3 | 5. How did they arrive at this equation? <br> 6. Do you see how it follows? <br> 7. Does it make sense? How did they get this? |
| To find G, substitute 36 1/3 for B in either equation. We use equation (2). | 8. Do this, then we'll read the next part. |
| G = 2B <br> = 2 × 36 1/3 <br> = 72 2/3 | |
| So the solution is (B, G) = (36 1/3, 72 2/3). The Boy Scouts will receive $36.33, and the Girl Scouts will get $72.67. | 9. Did you get the same result? |
| *Check* | |
| Are both conditions satisfied? | 10. What conditions do they mean here? |
| Will the groups receive a total of $109? Yes, $36.33 + $72.67 = $109. Will the boys get twice as much as the girls? Yes, it is as close as possible. | 11. How would you show this? <br> Where did they get this equation? |

*Note:* Text in the left column above is adapted from *University of Chicago School Mathematics Project: Algebra* (p. 536), by J. McConnell et al., 1990, Glenview, IL: Scott Foresman.

Guided reading is best done in small groups, with the teacher encouraging students to think of their own questions as they read. A predetermined set of questions isn't necessary. The purpose of guided reading is to help students realize that they can engage with and make sense of the text, whether it be in language arts or mathematics.

# Conclusion

Mathematics teachers don't need to become reading specialists in order to help students read mathematics texts, but they do need to recognize that students need their help reading in mathematical contexts. Teachers should make the strategic processes necessary for understanding mathematics explicit to students. Teachers must help students use strategies for acquiring vocabulary and reading word problems for meaning. Students are helped not by having their reading and interpreting done for them, but rather by being asked questions when they don't understand the text. The goal is for students to internalize these questions and use them on their own.

Mathematics teachers are ultimately striving to help their students understand mathematics and to use it in all aspects of their lives. Being aware that students' prior knowledge and background affects their comprehension is vastly important, as is explicitly analyzing the organization of mathematics texts. When we share strategies for understanding text, question our students about their conceptual processes, and model strategies and questioning techniques, we are helping students to develop metacognitive processes for approaching mathematics tasks. Mathematics teachers should recognize that part of their job in helping their students become autonomous, self-directed learners is first to help them become strategic, facile readers of mathematics text.

# 3

# Writing in the Mathematics Classroom

*Cynthia L. Tuttle*

Dave has taught mathematics for twelve years. Before that, he had been an accountant, but he felt he wasn't doing enough with his life, so he went back to college to be certified as a teacher. When hired to teach 7th grade, he threw himself into his work, applying all his organizational talents to the classroom. He kept track of the skills and concepts that he needed to teach and monitored each student's progress. Over time, he became a resource to the other mathematics teachers because of his content knowledge (he was certified to teach through 12th grade), his organization, and his understanding of mathematics in the real world.

Despite his success, Dave was disappointed in his students' struggles with a unit on fractions, decimals, and percentages. He decided to put extra time into the unit during the first half of the year, and to review the material in warm-ups—five- to ten-minute practice sessions at the beginning of each class—the rest of the year. He insisted that the students who struggled the most work with him after school. Yet when the state assessment scores came out, Dave was dismayed—many of his students did not do well on questions involving fractions, decimals, and percentages. He discussed the results with his principal and colleagues and attributed his students' low scores to their poor attitudes toward mathematics, their low work ethic, and their unwillingness to do homework.

---

*Note:* This chapter contains material that has been released to the public by the Massachusetts Department of Education. The Department of Education has not endorsed the material contained in this chapter.

The next year, Dave had the opportunity to become an 8th grade teacher. He jumped at the chance to teach "harder" mathematics; he also thought he would have a head start with the students, as he had taught most of them the previous year. Dave opened the year with a pretest to identify students' strengths and weaknesses. When he corrected the pretests, he found that the students with whom he had worked so diligently the year before had forgotten much of what they'd "learned" about fractions, decimals, and percentages. He was again baffled and discouraged. Despite his conscientious teaching, the students were not retaining the material or successfully applying it to new situations.

It's not unusual for mathematics teachers to become frustrated because their students were not well-enough prepared in earlier grades for what they must now learn. Talk to the prior mathematics teachers, and they will maintain that they did what they could. So the question becomes: If students have been taught the material and haven't learned or retained it, what can we as professionals do to change the scenario?

In searching for answers to this question, I began to investigate the role of writing in the mathematics classroom. For me, writing has always been important to my learning; I write out everything from professional workshop presentations to lists of what I want to discuss with the doctor. Writing in this way slows down and focuses my thinking; I am able to hear each word in my head and see it on paper. It is like a *mindful meditation* during which I shut out the rest of the world and am totally engaged in the process.

Another benefit of writing is that it allows the page to become a holding place for our thoughts until we can build upon them. We can revisit our written thoughts as often as needed and thus revise our thinking. Although I start with an overall plan when I write, I do not know where the ideas and words will take me until the process of writing drags them out of me—much as many artists do not know where a picture is going until the paint touches the canvas.

# Linguistic Versus Logical-Mathematical Intelligence

Throughout life, we try to make sense of the world using the four skills of listening, speaking, reading, and writing. According to Howard Gardner (1983), these skills make up our linguistic intelligence and form the basis for much of our school achievement. There is, however, another intelligence that also affects our achievement in school: logical-mathematical intelligence. The main difference between these two intelligences, notes Gardner, is that linguistic intelligence is not closely tied to the realm of physical objects, whereas logical-mathematical intelligence is primarily rooted in the material world. Both types of intelligences have been the focus of most "achievement" testing in the United States.

Traditionally, linguistic intelligence has been considered more important than logical-mathematical intelligence. Students with poor linguistic intelligence are often considered less capable than their peers and are placed in lower-level groups or classes. If this practice continues through secondary school, it begins to limit the type of higher education available to the struggling students. As adults, many of them will be forced to devise involved strategies to hide their literacy problems.

Failure in mathematics does not carry as severe a stigma. In some circles, it is viewed in the same way as not being able to carry a tune—lamentable, but not overly significant. However, as our economy becomes more and more technology-based, an imperfect sense of mathematical pitch can have serious ramifications. As with their literacy-challenged peers, students who do not do well in mathematics are often placed in lower groups or classes, thus restricting their future academic choices. Fortunately, some of this is starting to change. Mathematics is beginning to be viewed less as a series of arithmetic calculations than as "the science of order, patterns, structure, and logical relationships" (Devlin, 2000).

## Changing Perceptions and New Expectations

In its *Principles and Standards for School Mathematics* (2000), the National Council of Teachers of Mathematics (NCTM) directs that mathematics programs be designed so that all students can succeed. Whereas mathematics used to be viewed as a narrow topic with limited student success rates, it is now conceived as broad and requiring the understanding of *all* students. This is a momentous change of perception, and an equally momentous challenge for educators.

As Zinsser stresses in his book *Writing to Learn* (1989), it is important that all students be involved in the mathematics classroom. Twenty-five students cannot all speak at the same time, but they can all write at the same time, and writing encourages them to become engaged in their learning.

I will never forget a parent-teacher conference early in my career. The student under discussion had scored poorly in mathematics; though he could hold all the big ideas in his head, he struggled mightily when it came to computation. For some reason, he just couldn't get the numbers on paper correctly. I knew I had to share these difficulties with his parents, who I suspected had heard this chronicle of failure before. I desperately wanted him to succeed—of all my students, he displayed the greatest discrepancy between achievement in computation and understanding of mathematics concepts. As I started to describe his progress so far, his mother interrupted me and said, "Oh, don't worry about his mathematics. I was the same way in school, and now I manage a $7 million budget just fine." I have thought a lot about her comment since then, and my reflection invariably leads to the question of why can't we make students like this one as successful in "school math" as they may become in later life.

Fortunately, mathematics content and pedagogy are changing. The expanded content that emphasizes solving real-world problems would have held great appeal for my calculation-poor, concept-rich student. If his mathematics work had involved more writing, he would have been better able to emphasize his conceptual strength and resolve his computational difficulties (with the aid of a two-dollar, four-function calculator if necessary!). Written explanations in mathematics are about *what* is being done and *why* it works. The type of thinking involved in justifying a strategy or explaining an answer is quite different from that needed to merely solve an equation. *The process of writing about a mathematics problem will itself often lead to a solution.*

## Written Responses to Mathematics Problems

Early in their schooling, many students are introduced to response logs in language arts class (Maloch, 2002). In their logs, students write comments and questions about what they have read before engaging in small-group discussions. This practice gives all students the opportunity *and* responsibility to interact with what they've read. The same experience can be provided in mathematics class. Once students have done some initial writing about a problem, they can share their strategies in small groups. In attempting to solve the problem, the students will have additional opportunities for writing. Following each group's report, the teacher may present a related writing assignment.

If students begin the problem on their own, they are starting from their own mathematical way of thinking. Bringing their written solutions to the small group helps students investigate mathematics more deeply. There are many ways that students may respond to this problem. Figure 3.1 shows an example of a basic problem that a teacher might give to students to assess their understanding of the factors of 32, along with four different ways that students might approach it.

| FIGURE 3.1 | Four Possible Written Responses to a Mathematics Problem |
| --- | --- |

**The Problem**
Four students could not go on a field trip. They had paid $32 in total for their tickets. How much money was returned to each student?

**Directions to the Student**
1. Read the problem.
2. Write down one possible strategy to solve the problem. Use diagrams or pictures when possible.
3. Write down any questions you have about the problem.

**Possible Response #1**

| Student #1 | Student #2 | Student #3 | Student #4 |
| --- | --- | --- | --- |
| $5 | $5 | $5 | $5 |
| $2 | $2 | $2 | $2 |
| $1 | $1 | $1 | $1 |
| $8 | $8 | $8 | $8 |

I knew that each student could not get $10 because 4 x $10 = $40, so I returned $5 to each student for a total of $20 (4 x $5 = $20). I had $12 left ($32 - $20 = $12). I gave each student $2 (4 x $2 = $8). I had $4 left ($12 - $8 = $4). I gave each student $1 (4 x $1 = $4), and I had returned all the money ($4 - $4 = $0). Each student received $8 back.

**Possible Response #2**

I knew that $32 had to be shared equally among four students.
$32 – $4 = $28   Each student received $1.
$28 – $4 = $24   Each student received $1.
$24 – $4 = $20   Each student received $1.
$20 – $4 = $16   Each student received $1.
$16 – $4 = $12   Each student received $1.
$12 – $4 = $8    Each student received $1.
$8 – $4 = $4     Each student received $1.
$4 – $4 = $0     Each student received $1.
All the money has been returned. Each student has received a total of $8.

*(Figure continues on next page)*

| FIGURE 3.1 | Four Possible Written Responses to a Mathematics Problem *(Continued)* |
|---|---|

**Possible Response #3**

I knew that $32 had to be shared equally among four students, so I gave each student $1 until all my bills were gone. I gave out $4 at a time.

Time 1: ($1 + $1 + $1 + $1)
Time 2: ($1 + $1 + $1 + $1)
Time 3: ($1 + $1 + $1 + $1)
Time 4: ($1 + $1 + $1 + $1)
Time 5: ($1 + $1 + $1 + $1)
Time 6: ($1 + $1 + $1 + $1)
Time 7: ($1 + $1 + $1 + $1)
Time 8: ($1 + $1 + $1 + $1)

I gave out $4 ($1 + $1 + $1 + $1) at a time.
$4 + $4 + $4 + $4 + $4 + $4 + $4 + $4.
I gave out $4 eight times. Each student received $8.

**Possible Response #4**

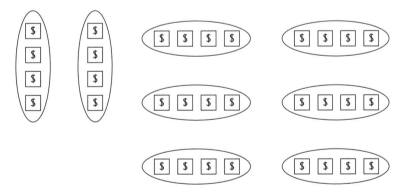

I gave out $1 at a time to each of the four students. All together, I have eight groups of $4. That means each student received $1 eight times for a total of $8.

By the time the students have finished studying a problem like the one in Figure 3.1, they have looked at it in depth, first from their own perspective and then from the perspectives of others. Students need to untangle what is in their own minds first, get it on paper, and then share their thinking with others. This ensures that there will be a wide range of responses to each question.

Students absorb mathematics from their peers when they share these responses with each other. After viewing other student responses, the students can be encouraged to generate additional possible solutions. To quote Stigler and Hiebert (1999):

> When this type of learning experience is used, the range of individual differences will be revealed. Individual differences are beneficial for the class because they produce a wide range of ideas and solution methods that provide the material for students' discussion and reflection. The variety of alternative methods allows students to compare them and construct connections among them. It is believed that all students benefit from the variety of ideas generated by their peers. (p. 94)

Mathematics writing requires hard work and planning on the part of the teacher and takes time and practice to develop properly. Teachers who facilitate this type of learning know their students well and can anticipate possible responses based on their students' prior ones. New variations will likely emerge as students reflect on the solutions of their classmates.

In order for mathematics writing to be effective, the following guidelines must be observed:

• The problem must be appropriate for the students who are going to be writing about it.

• The students must know how to use blocks, diagrams, pictures, or grids to work out their solutions before writing about them.

• The students must have confidence in their ability to respond to the problem as individuals. They must think of themselves as successful mathematics learners.

• The students must feel comfortable sharing their answers without fear of being ridiculed. This means that the teacher and other students have to accept all responses as worthy of discussion.

• The problem must be discussed with the whole class, and all strategies must be reported.

## Additional Writing Strategies

All writing provides valuable opportunities for rewriting as a learning strategy. Students can develop their written responses more fully using cues from classmates or the teacher. This process gives students more time, and thus a deeper connection, with the subject. Other writing-to-learn strategies include journal keeping, creating problems similar to the one being solved, and directed expository writing. Fisher (2002) notes that resources are now available to help teachers guide the process of student writing about mathematical thinking. Once such writing is completed, students' responses should be arranged in a three-ring binder by category: class notes, developing vocabulary, homework, formal and informal assessments, and journal writing. The binder provides a written record of students' thinking and real learning.

Remember that this chapter began with a true story that supports the well-known observation that students don't remember what they learn in mathematics. Writing down what they've learned forces students to learn the material; as the adage goes, you don't really understand something until you can explain it to others. It no longer suffices for students to respond, "I don't know how I got the answer, I just know it." They are expected to scaffold the answer for the audience—the teacher and the other students—in a way that explains the answer. This is a controversial point of view. Parents, students, and even some teachers may balk at having to explain how they derived their answers. A correct response is all that is necessary in their minds. In today's mathematics classroom, the expectation is that all students, even those who instantly know the answer, should be able to justify their responses.

In other words, teachers should use writing to engage students in mathematics thinking at the outset of a lesson and continue asking them to put their thinking in writing throughout the lesson to refine their thinking. As we will see in the next section, this process allows teachers to see the *why*, not just the *how*, of the student's thinking.

# Writing as a Prerequisite for Assessment of Student Learning

The objective of any mathematics lesson is for students to be able to apply some aspect of mathematical thinking. Writing provides unique evidence teachers can use to assess student mathematics skills. The answer to a problem alone does not tell teachers *how* students are learning: even if the answer is correct (and assuming that the student did the work independently), the strategy the student followed is unknown. If the answer is incorrect, the teacher does not know at what point the student's thinking led to an incorrect response. As the NCTM (2000) states,

Many assessment techniques can be used by mathematics teachers, including open-ended questions, constructed-response tasks, selected response items, performance tasks, observations, conversations, journals, and portfolios. These methods can all be appropriate for classroom assessment, but some may apply more readily to particular goals. For example, quizzes using simple constructed-response or selected-response items may indicate whether students can apply procedures. Constructed response or performance tasks may better illuminate students' capacity to apply mathematics in complex or new situations. Observations and conversations in the classroom can provide insights into students' thinking, and teachers can monitor changes in students' thinking and reasoning over time with reflective journals and portfolios. (pp. 23–24)

Writing not only provides a measure of student performance, but also suggests to the teacher what type of learning experience to present next. Where are the students in the learning of the material? What should the next lesson have as its objective? What can I learn from my students' partially correct approaches? What must the students understand before we can progress? These are all questions that can be answered by reviewing student writing.

Teachers can further assess student mathematics knowledge by asking open-ended questions. Responses to questions such as "What is division?" reveal whether or not the students have learned the subject procedurally or conceptually. These types of exercises are helpful both in the early and later grades. If students are familiar with mathematics writing at the elementary level, the transition to secondary school will seem natural. If not, teachers will need to familiarize the students with the process. If a standards-based curriculum is in place, daily open-ended questions should already be built into it.

Educators have slowly come to acknowledge the importance of open-ended questions in preparing students for high-stakes tests. Also useful are anchor papers from previous years that provide samples of student writing. Studying these papers—examining the mathematics involved, discussing the pedagogy, and reviewing responses—helps teachers practice viewing writing as evidence of learning.

Figure 3.2 shows an open-response question that appeared on a recent 8th grade high-stakes assessment test. Think about solving this problem yourself. Would you first draw four black tiles and surround them with white tiles so that you could count the number of white tiles? Would you make a table? Would you use the table to determine the number of white tiles necessary for

---

| FIGURE 3.2 | Sample Open-Ended Problem from an 8th Grade Test |

A worker placed white tiles around black tiles in the pattern shown in the three figures below:

 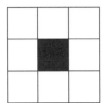 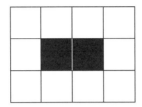 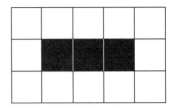

a. Based on this pattern, how many white tiles would be needed for 4 black tiles?

b. Based on this pattern, how many white tiles would be needed for 50 black tiles?

c. Make a scatter plot of the first five figures in this pattern showing the relationship between the number of white tiles and the number of black tiles. Be sure to label the axes.

d. Based on this pattern, explain how you could find the number of white tiles needed for any number, *n*, of black tiles. Show and explain your work.

*Source:* From *Release of Spring 2002 Test Items* (question #9), by the Massachusetts Department of Education, 2002, Malden, MA: Author. Reprinted by permission.

---

50 black tiles? Would you use the table to develop the equation? Are you able to make a scatter plot with the axes labeled?

Now compare your approach with the student papers shown in Figures 3.3–3.6. As the responses in these figures make clear, the students are required to apply their skills, prove their solutions, draw generalizations, and make connections using words as well as diagrams—all categories of thinking that are classified at the higher end of commonly held educational objectives. This type of standards-based assessment helps students develop confidence in their mathematical thinking and clearly provides much more information for the assessor than would a single answer on a multiple-choice test.

## Additional Strategies

In order to tap into their prior knowledge, students need to organize whatever they are writing about. This is particularly important in developing mathematics vocabulary. The guidelines of the Connected Mathematics Project (Lappan, 2002) recommend that students record new words as they initially understand

| FIGURE 3.3 | Sample Response to Tile Problem—#1 |
|---|---|

a. For a pattern with 4 black tiles you would need 14 white tiles.

b. For a pattern with 50 black tiles you would need 106 white tiles.

d. To find the number of white tiles for any number you could use the formula below

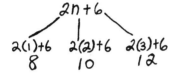

$2n+6$

$2(1)+6$    $2(2)+6$    $2(3)+6$
$8$        $10$        $12$

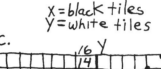

X = black tiles
Y = white tiles

c.

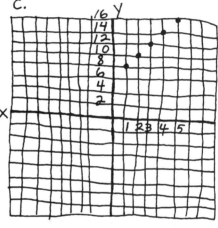

**AUTHOR COMMENT**

*In this example, the student correctly answers the number of white tiles for 4 black tiles and 50 black tiles, shows a scatter plot of the first five tiles, and provides an expression that can be used to determine the number of white tiles for any number of black tiles.*

Source: Student responses in Figures 3.3–3.6 from *Release of Spring 2002 Test Items* (question #9), by the Massachusetts Department of Education, 2002, Malden, MA: Author. Reprinted by permission.

their meaning from the context in which they are used. For example, students may have a lesson in which they place one-inch squares within a rectangular figure:

| FIGURE 3.4 | Sample Response to Tile Problem—#2 |
|---|---|

A. 14 white tiles would be needed for four black tiles.

B. 106 white tiles would be needed to make 50 black tiles

C.
$$2b+b$$
$1$ black tile $= 8$ white tiles      $3$ black tiles $= 12$ white tiles

$2$ black tiles $= 10$ white tiles      $4$ black tiles $= 14$ white tiles

$5$ black tiles $= 16$ white tiles

d. $n = 2b + b$      $B = $ black, $n = $ white

It took a lot of thought to find this formula. I looked at the white and black tiles closely for quite a while. In all the patterns, there was 12 times the number of black tiles, plus 6. This formula works for every pattern of black and white tiles.

**AUTHOR COMMENT**

*In this example, the student answers correctly the number of white tiles necessary to surround 4 black tiles and 50 black tiles and partially describes a pattern that can be used to find the number of white tiles necessary to surround any number of black tiles. However, the response does not show a scatter plot.*

The students can then count the number of placed squares and record the area either as "eight square inches" or as "eight-inch squares." Their next assignment could be to write their own definition of the word *area*. At this point, a student might write, "Area is the number of one-inch squares that fit inside a rectangle." With subsequent lessons, students can further develop this initial definition to include other measures (standard and metric) and shapes. Different ways of determining the area and eventually computing it evolve through multiple experiences with the word *area* and its definition. Vocabulary so developed

| FIGURE 3.5 | Sample Response to Tile Problem—#3 |
| --- | --- |

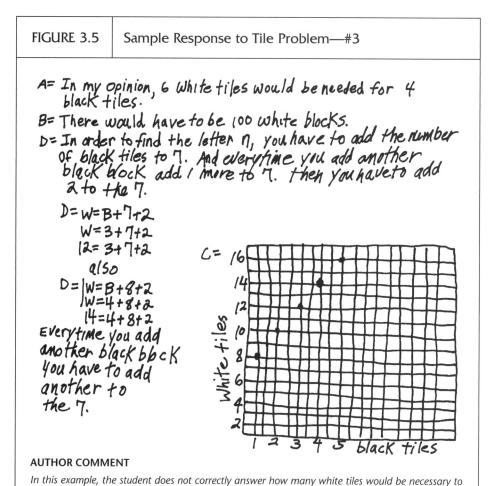

A= In my opinion, 6 white tiles would be needed for 4 black tiles.

B= There would have to be 100 white blocks.

D= In order to find the letter n, you have to add the number of black tiles to 7. And everytime you add another black block add 1 more to 7. then you have to add 2 to the 7.

$$D = W = B + 7 + 2$$
$$W = 3 + 7 + 2$$
$$12 = 3 + 7 + 2$$

also

$$D = \begin{vmatrix} W = B + 8 + 2 \\ W = 4 + 8 + 2 \\ 14 = 4 + 8 + 2 \end{vmatrix}$$

Everytime you add another black bbcK you have to add another to the 7.

**AUTHOR COMMENT**

*In this example, the student does not correctly answer how many white tiles would be necessary to surround 4 black tiles and 50 black tiles. However, the scatter plot is correct. The student does not provide the general pattern for finding the number of black tile needed.*

becomes learned. One system of organizing this vocabulary is to have a sheet of paper for each letter of the alphabet with student-derived definitions. This "dictionary" can be transferred to the next year's class for continuation.

As the NCTM (2000) notes,

It is important to give students experiences that help them appreciate the power and precision of mathematical language. Beginning in the middle grades, students should understand the role of mathematical definitions

| FIGURE 3.6 | Sample Response to Tile Problem—#4 |
|---|---|

a. 12 white tiles would be needed for four black tiles.

b. 150 white tiles would be needed for 50 black tiles

c. I. [diagram] 8 white tiles, 1 black tile    II. [diagram] 10 w. tiles, 2 black tiles

III. [diagram] 12 w. tiles, 3 b. tiles    IV. [diagram] 14 w. tiles, 4 b. tiles

IV. [diagram] 16 w. tiles, 5 b. tiles

d. I could find out the # of tiles needed for every 1 black tile easily. For everyone tile there are two other white tiles. For the first one you need to surround it with tiles. Then everytime you add a black one you add two white ones.

**AUTHOR COMMENT**

*In this example, the student does not show the correct response for the number of white tiles needed to surround 4 black tiles or 50 black tiles and does not show a scatter plot. However, the diagrams for the number of white tiles necessary to surround 1, 2, 3, 4, and 5 black tiles are correct, and the labels for each diagram are correct. There is an indication that the student is beginning to notice a pattern: "every time you add a black one you add two white ones."*

and should use them in mathematical work. Doing so should become pervasive in high school. However, it is important to avoid a premature rush to impose formal mathematical language; students need to develop an appreciation of the need for precise definitions and for the communicative power of conventional mathematical terms by first communicating in their own words. Allowing students to grapple with their ideas and develop their own informal means of expressing them can be an effective way to foster engagement and ownership. (p. 63)

Providing a structured guide for their writing can be particularly helpful for students. In one urban district, 6th graders responded positively to the structured writing guide in Figure 3.7, which the teacher revised as needed.

| FIGURE 3.7 | Sample Structured Writing Guide |
| --- | --- |

**Paragraph One: Problem Statement**

Write answers to these two questions:
- What is the problem about?
- What am I supposed to find?

**Paragraph Two: Work Write-Up**

Explain step-by-step and in detail everything you did to arrive at each of your answers. Think of this as a recipe for someone to follow or as directions to your house. Complete the following sentences:
- First I . . .
- Then I . . .
- Next I . . .
- After that I . .
- Finally I . . .

**Paragraph Three: Answer**

Prove that your answer is correct by referring to the math you did. Do *not* write that you checked it on the calculator, you did it twice, or your friend told you it looked OK. Complete the following sentences:
- My answer is . . .
- My answer makes sense because . . .

*Source:* From *Guide for Writing Response in Mathematics*, by L. Jubinville, unpublished manuscript, 2002. Reprinted with permission.

# Mathematics Writing and ESL Students

Research at California State University indicates that some aspects of learning a second language are similar to learning a first language, and occur naturally with a shift to a new language environment. Beyond this natural learning, however, direct instruction is necessary. The grammatical items that tend to cause the most difficulty for English-as-a-second-language (ESL) students are count and noncount nouns, articles, prepositions, tense, and vocabulary. When students do not know the word they need in the second language, they must find ways to write around it. Describing processes and concepts is a huge challenge for ESL students; strategies such as maintaining a vocabulary log, prewriting, editing, and revising can help (California State University Writing Center, 2003).

There is some debate as to whether or not students should be verbally fluent before they begin to write. According to Nekita Lamour of the Hood Children's Literacy Project (2003), students should be able to write in their own language first and have it translated into the new language. (Initially someone else should translate the writing; as the students' writing skills develop, they may translate their work themselves and have it edited.) Lamour also feels it is important that students continue to develop as speakers in their native language.

All students, regardless of their language or cultural background, must study a core curriculum in mathematics based on the NCTM standards. For students to truly develop mathematics literacy, however, lessons must be based on real-life experience, involve problem solving, and occur in an environment in which students hear, speak, and write mathematics language. For ESL students, teachers must focus on their skills both in mathematics language and in English. For example, if the students are working with obtuse angles, they need to understand the meaning of the suffix -er in "greater than." They also need to understand the connection between angles in mathematics class and angles as discussed in science and social studies classes. Teachers should initially keep language simple, particularly if the concept being discussed is hard to grasp. It is beneficial if the English and mathematics teachers of ESL students train and work together regularly. Teacher intervention is more important than repetition and drills; this is as important for ESL learners as it is for regular-track students.

# The Cognitive Academic Language Learning Approach

The Cognitive Academic Language Learning Approach (CALLA) for Mathematics and Science provides support for ESL learners in both content and learning strategies (Spanos, 1993). Figure 3.8 shows three strategies developed by CALLA to help students solve problems successfully. Though specifically designed with ESL learners in mind, these strategies are also applicable to all students.

| FIGURE 3.8 | Three CALLA Strategies |
|---|---|

**#1: Word Problem Procedure**
1. Choose a partner or partners.
2. Choose a problem and write it out.
3. Have one student read the problem out loud. Discuss the vocabulary and circle words you don't understand.
4. Use a dictionary or partner for help, and write out the definitions of the vocabulary words you did not understand.
5. Write out what the problem is asking you to find.
6. Consider what process you should use to solve the problem. Should you add? Subtract? Multiply? Divide?
7. Solve the problem.
8. Check your answer.
9. Explain your answer to your partner.
10. Write your explanation.
11. Explain your answer to the class.
12. Write a similar problem on a piece of paper.

**#2: Mathematics Learning Strategy Checklist**
*There are many ways to solve problems. Check the two or three things that you did most while you worked on this problem. There are no right or wrong answers.*

☐ I looked for the important words to solve the problem.

☐ I read the question carefully.

☐ I remembered how I solved other problems like this one.

☐ I did the problem in my head because it was easy.

☐ I formed a picture in my head or drew a picture.

**#3: Math Student Self-Evaluation**
These are two important things I learned in math today/this week/this month:

1. _____

_____

*(Figure continues on next page)*

Using student writing as evidence for assessment purposes is particularly important with ESL students. Figure 3.9 depicts part of an assessment problem from an 8th grade ESL class. Envision that the teacher writes a response to each answer in order to encourage students to think more deeply about the question and to write down more of their thinking.

| FIGURE 3.8 | Three CALLA Strategies *(Continued)* |
| --- | --- |

2. _____

_____

This was an easy problem for me: _____

_____

This was a difficult problem for me: _____

_____

I need more help with: _____

This is how I feel about math today/this week/this month (circle the words that are true):

*successful*              *happy*                *excited*

*confused*               *interested*            *worried*

*relaxed*                *bored*                *upset*

This is where I got help (circle the words that are true):

*my teacher*

*my friend or classmate*

*my parents*

*Source:* From *ESL Math and Science for High School Students,* by G. Spanos, paper presented at the 3rd National Research Symposium on Limited English Proficient Student Issues, 1993, Washington, DC: National Clearinghouse for English Language Acquisition.

Here are some examples of the students' answers, each with the accompanying teacher response:

**Student 1:** By looking at the graph, you can tell Anne is going the same speed because it shows every 6 miles: 6, 12, 18, 24, 30, 36 miles. And there is a straight line. It never is a flat line.

**Teacher:** What can you say about the distance Anne travels each hour?

_____

| FIGURE 3.9 | Sample Assessment Problem from an ESL Class |
| --- | --- |

**Bicycle Rides**

The Liberty Bicycle Path is 36 miles long. The following graph describes Anne's ride along the bike path one afternoon between 3 p.m. and 6 p.m. How can you tell from the graph that Anne was riding at the same speed for the whole trip?

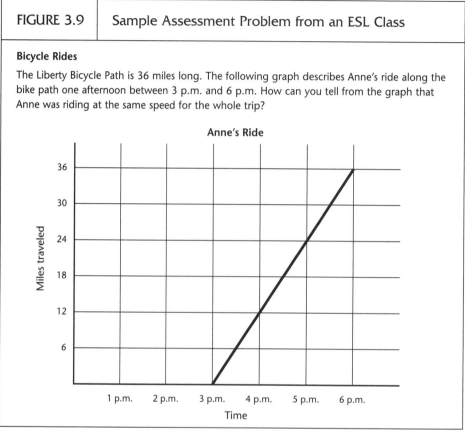

*Source:* From *Balanced Mathematics Assessment for the 21st Century* (p. 84), by J. L. Schwartz et al., 2000, Cambridge, MA: Harvard Graduate School of Education. Reprinted with permission.

**Student 2:** She stays in one time period, and she goes fast.
**Teacher:** How do you know she is going fast?

———————

**Student 3:** You can tell because each goes by 6. She took 6 miles to get over there at 6:00 p.m.
**Teacher:** What do you notice about how many miles Anne traveled between 3 p.m. and 4 p.m.?

———————

**Student 4:** I can tell from the graph that Anne was riding at the same speed because she was going straight up not stopping. But she wasn't going the same speed because the more she goes up the more the speed she goes.

**Teacher:** Why is the line straight between 3 p.m. and 4 p.m.? How far did Anne travel during that time? Why is the line straight between 4 p.m. and 5 p.m.? How far did Anne travel during that time? Why is the line straight between 5 p.m. and 6 p.m.? How far did Anne travel during that time?

---

**Student 5:** Because each hour she traveled 12 miles.

**Teacher:** In what other ways can you explain Anne's speed using the information on this graph?

---

**Student 6:** Because the miles increase 6 miles, then 12 miles, then 18 miles, then 24 each.

**Teacher:** What do you notice about the number of miles Anne travels and the amount of time she has been riding?

---

**Student 7:** You look at how straight the line is and how much the miles were for every hour and check if it's the same as the last.

**Teacher:** Why does the line look straight when you compare the miles traveled and the number of hours Anne had been riding?

---

**Student 8:** Because the line that connects the dots goes up in a straight line. It doesn't show that she stopped or went slower.

**Teacher:** Why does the information on the graph give this result?

---

**Student 9:** Because it is just going straight up like this (/) and not like this (/\/).

**Teacher:** What information on the graph makes the line stay straight? What would make it change direction?

---

The *bicycle rides* task required students to interpret a line graph in which the slope of the line represents speed. The process of teachers' responding to the initial student answers, and of the students' then responding in writing to the teacher's comments, cannot help but deepen and enrich the level of student understanding.

## Student Writing and Special Needs

Here is a real-world mathematics problem that I experienced recently.

One of the plastic spokes broke on my new umbrella. I returned it to the store with the sales slip, which recorded the original price of $22.00 and the marked-down price of $17.60. The sales clerk ran my credit card through the machine and said, "Oops! I charged you another $17.60. I'll do it again and credit you for returning two umbrellas."

The sales clerk proceeded to credit the two umbrellas (the one I had returned and the one for which she accidentally charged me). She entered into the machine "2 @ $17.50," marked down from $35, as a credit of $28.

The sales clerk brought me the slip. I was expecting "2 @ $17.60" to be a credit of $35.20. What kind of math made it $28? The original umbrella was $17.60 marked down from $22, for a 20 percent markdown. $28 is 20 percent off of $35, but the $35 was the total refund short 20 cents because the clerk had punched in $17.50 instead of $17.60. The clerk gave up and called a manager, who charged me $28 to counteract the $28 returned to me. She then credited me for two umbrellas at $17.60 each for a total of $35.20, and the transaction was complete.

Incidentally, the first transaction in the return of the umbrella occurred at 10:36 a.m. Subsequent entries were at 10:37 a.m., 10:50 a.m., and 10:52 a.m. It took 16 minutes to do the necessary mathematics so that I could be credited for a returned umbrella—an inordinate amount of wait time.

This is just one small example of how each of us faces mathematics problems every day. The point of the umbrella story is that, in the age of computers, everyone needs to be able to think mathematically in order to do such basic things as shop (or work in a shop). We live in a time when to hold most jobs probably involves some technology. However, it is not enough to just push the buttons; we also have to think about the mathematics behind our calculations.

For this reason, mathematics instruction must be customized to meet the varied learning styles of special-needs students. Take the case of Richard, who was identified early on in school as "developmentally delayed." He had trouble with recall and with memorizing rote facts. He hated mathematics and struggled with some basic arithmetic every school day until 6th grade.

Richard was in a self-contained special education program when he met a math teacher, Mr. D., who was excited about a standards-based mathematics program for middle school about which he had recently learned. Mr. D. not only was impressed by this program but also believed that, with modifications, Richard could succeed in using it. One of the first mathematics lessons that Mr. D. prepared for Richard was "The Factor Game." Among the game's objectives is learning that some numbers, such as 4, have only a few factors (1, 2, 4), whereas other numbers, such as 12, have many (1, 2, 3, 4, 6, 12).

Mr. D. had already ascertained that Richard had to compensate for his lack of multiplication skills by using addition. Richard would do manipulations such as $9 \times 8$ not from memory but through repeated addition. Mr. D. was impressed that Richard had an alternative strategy but saw it as time consuming, so he had Richard write out all the factors for the numbers from 1 to 30 to use in The Factor Game; Richard was also allowed to use a multiplication chart.

After doing as Mr. D. requested, Richard was able to learn what factors are and how to integrate them into his multiplication strategy. He learned new vocabulary and discovered that some numbers have more factors than others. Over time, Richard began to recall more of the multiplication facts and was eventually able to correctly answer factor-related questions on the end-of-the-year state assessment test. At the close of the school year, Richard moved to another community. Teachers, aides, and students gathered in a circle to bid him good-bye. Richard said he did not want to go to a new school because Mr. D. was the only teacher who had believed that he could do mathematics.

This story is touching because we know how important success is to any student's academic achievement. How many Richards are there who never get a chance to succeed in mathematics? How many of our students do not really understand what they are doing and are not developing into the mathematicians they could become?

Traditionally, many students have been labeled as poor performers in mathematics because they were not successful in computational arithmetic. Yet many of these students may be conceptually capable and can be successful at algebra, probability, and calculus. They are also different kinds of learners who have deficits in concrete representations. Much of the mathematics that frustrates these students is not complicated; it is just not amenable to memorization. The simple activity of scribing—be it words, numbers, or pictures—is particularly important to the development of mathematical understanding.

Also effective for special-needs students is the MATHPLAN program (Warren, 2002). It is informative to look at the structured writing prompts for two of the tasks from this collection (Figures 3.10 and 3.11).

| FIGURE 3.10 | MATHPLAN Task 1: "Where's the Car?" |

You and your mother go to the toy store. When you get there, you find that the parking spaces are numbered but some of the numbers have worn off the pavement. You need to help your mother remember where the car is located, but she has parked in a spot without a number.

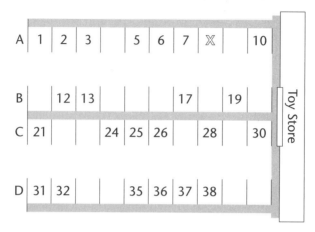

1. Use this map of the parking lot. (The X on the map is your car.)
   • Find the number of the space that your car is parked in.
   • Fill in the numbers of the other spaces that are not marked.
2. At the entrance to the store, you run into a friend and his dad. After you tell them where your car is, your friend's father says that they have parked three spaces away from you in the same aisle, but he doesn't tell you the number of their space. You want to know where they are because your friend has your baseball in the trunk of his car and you want to get it back.

   While your parents talk to each other, you and your friend go to get the ball and put it in your car. Using the aisle letters and space numbers, explain to your friend the fastest way (best route) to get the ball into your car and the two of you back to the store entrance.

**Instructions for the Teacher**

Copy the following fill-in-the-blank statements in whatever format the student is used to seeing, such as your handwriting with large print on lined paper, worksheet-type computer-printed pages, etc. Give the student the following statements to complete:

*It can't be in space #_____ because _____. We want to get to the cars as fast as*

*we can, so we should go to the end of Aisle _____ that is next to space #_____ and walk down the*

*aisle until we get to _____. We will have to _____ to put*

*the ball in my car, and then we can walk back to the door.*

*Source:* From *MATHPLAN: A Diagnostic and Prescriptive Collection for the Elementary Grades,* by A. R. Warren, unpublished manuscript, 2002. Reprinted with permission.

| FIGURE 3.11 | MATHPLAN Task 2: Block Sets |

You arrive at a part of the store where you can choose blocks of different shapes and colors to create your own sets. Your mother wants you to pick out sets of blocks for your three cousins, who are all about to have birthdays. She wants you to get a set of 20 blocks for Tommy and sets of 10 blocks each for Nancy and Natalie. Each set should have at least three different kinds of blocks.

These are the blocks you can choose from:

blue squares                                    orange triangles

red rectangles                                  green cylinders

1. How many blocks of each kind will you get for

  • Tommy?

  • Nancy?

  • Natalie?

2. What is the total number of each kind of block that you will get?

3. After you finish gathering all of the blocks, your mother remembers that she already has a gift for Tommy and asks you to put his blocks back into the bins. How many blocks of each kind will you have after you put the blocks for Tommy back? How do you know?

**Instructions for the Teacher**
Copy the following fill-in-the-blank statements in whatever format the student is most used to seeing, such as your handwriting with large print on lined paper, worksheet-type computer-printed pages, etc. Give the student the following statement to complete:

*I will have _____ blue squares, _____ red rectangles, _____ orange triangles,*

*and _____ green cylinders. I know this because _____ .*

*Source:* From *MATHPLAN: A Diagnostic and Prescriptive Collection for the Elementary Grades,* by A. R. Warren, unpublished manuscript, 2002. Reprinted with permission.

One of the most common deficits shared by special-needs students is a lack of organizational skills. In order to help them organize their thinking, and ultimately their writing, a structured-response guide is of high value. As student performance improves, the guides can offer less direction and allow greater latitude for the writing exercise.

# Writing Supports

Students in any class are in transition. Their papers in mathematics class are working drafts. Students who have not been able to use writing to explain their thinking now have technological supports, in the form of voice-activation software such as DragonDictate for Windows and Dragon Naturally Speaking (Software Maintenance, Inc.), ViaVoice (IBM), and Voice Express (L&H) (Educational Development Corp., 2001).

Voice activation software is designed for students who have difficulty writing by hand and processing text. In regular as well as special education classes, there are students who can say their thoughts but can't write them without feeling mentally overloaded. Voice activation software strengthens the reading and writing skills of students. Students begin by reading five or six passages into a microphone attached to a computer, to get the computer accustomed to their voices. If they can't read, then the students need to listen to the passages on tape and repeat them, one sentence at a time, into the computer. As the students say the words, the words appear on the screen. Over time, students will see sentences that don't represent what they meant to say and will be increasingly able to self-correct.

For students who have developed the mechanics of writing but have difficulty with organization, software programs such as Inspiration (Inspiration Software, Inc.) can help. Traditionally, students are taught to write first a topic sentence for their main idea, then an introduction, followed by an account of what happened, and then a conclusion. Many students cannot hold this organizational framework in their heads; others are just anxious to get the assignment done as quickly as possible. The Inspiration program encourages students to brainstorm all their ideas, visually connect them with arrows, and add thoughts to each idea. At the end of the process, the computer produces an outline from which the students can develop a paper. Even students for whom organization is a relatively automatic process will find that brainstorming and connecting ideas challenge their deepest thinking.

For example, let's assume a student is asked to summarize what he knows about the sums and products of odd and even numbers, as well as to justify his response. The student might use Inspiration by typing his thoughts into individual bubbles, represented here by bullets:

- "2 + 2 = 4. An even number plus an even number equals an even number. I tried this with square tiles, and every square tile could be paired with another square tile."

- "2 + 3 = 5. An even number plus an odd number equals an odd number. I tried this with square tiles, and there was one tile left over."
- "3 + 3 = 6. An odd number plus an odd number equals an even number. I tried this with square tiles, and every square tile could be paired with another square tile."

Arrows can then be drawn on the computer to connect each bubble, and an outline can be printed from which the student may compose an answer.

One helpful resource for teachers to consider is the Technology-Enhanced Learning Environment Web site, the stated goal of which is to provide motivational, cognitive, and metacognitive support to emergent as well as proficient writers (http://ott.educ.msu.edu/newott/projects/teleweb.asp). Both high- and low-tech solutions are available to help students organize their thoughts and their work by using flow charts, task analysis, webbing or networking, and outlining. Still, teachers must be cautioned that any piece of software can be incorrectly used, leading to students' memorizing the programs as opposed to expressing their own thinking. It is also important to note that these technological supports are relatively new. Though some of the technologies may initially be difficult to use with young children, as they continue to develop and teachers use them more often, they will probably play an enhanced role in the learning process.

## Summary

*Students who have opportunities, encouragement, and support for . . . writing in the mathematics classes reap dual benefits: they communicate to learn mathematics, and they learn to communicate mathematically.*
                    —National Council of Teachers of Mathematics (2000, p. 60)

Writing in mathematics helps students think. Students are confused when they are asked to talk about mathematics, and are afraid of giving an incorrect answer—but as long as strict guidelines for clarity and completeness are applied to student writing, there should be no "incorrect" answers. Writing in mathematics allows students time to wonder and to process. It encourages them to address the more conceptual level of mathematics, not as rote learning, but as higher-level thinking.

By recording their thinking about mathematics problems, students help explain the solutions—and the process of *arriving* at a solution helps to *develop* the solution. Writing clarifies what it is the problems are asking. In order to justify their solutions, student writers are forced to think through, and find the meaning in, their responses.

Student writing helps teachers determine the type of learning that is occurring, informs them as to whether or not the students understand the lesson objectives, and reveals the level of understanding behind the students' algorithmic computations. The students' ability to justify solutions, notice patterns, and draw generalizations should be evident in their writing, as should their readiness to apply lessons learned to new problems.

Writing in the mathematics classroom serves two purposes: as a medium for students to develop their mathematical thinking and as a guide for teachers to use as they assess and plan. Learning mathematics without explicit writing severely limits the depth of communication that can be achieved between teacher and learner.

# 4

# Graphic Representation in the Mathematics Classroom

*Loretta Heuer*

What comes to mind when you see $\Delta$? Do you see the shape literally, as a triangle? Or do you assign a symbolic meaning to it, perhaps assuming it is related to finding the slope of a line?

What does the word *base* conjure up for you when it's used in mathematics? Is your first instinct a numeric one in our familiar base-10 system, or perhaps in systems based on other numbers such as 4 or 12? Or do you think of *base* as part of a geometric figure? Did you envision the base of a polygon, which would be a line? Or of a polyhedron, which would be an area?

And what about the word *or* in that last sentence? Was I using the term conversationally, or mathematically? And, if mathematically, did I intend it to be the inclusive *or* or the exclusive *or* (Hersh, 1997)?

No wonder students get befuddled!

The following aspects of mathematical language are particularly confusing to students:

• Technical symbols such as $\Sigma$, $\leq$, or $\Delta$. These signs, also known as logograms, stand for whole words but have no sound-symbol relationship for students to decode.

• Technical vocabulary—words such as *rhombus, hypotenuse,* and *integer,* which are rarely used in everyday conversation.

• The assignment of special definitions to familiar words such as *similar* and *prime*.

• Subtle morphology (one *hundred, hundreds*-place, *hundredths*) and the use of "little words" (prepositions, pronouns, articles, and conjunctions) in a technical syntax so precise that meaning is often obscured rather than clarified.

But mathematics is not only composed of words and symbols. It is also a pictorial language that uses visual models to communicate. How teachers use the language of pictures and diagrams to communicate with students and check for understanding is the subject of this chapter.

The following scenarios involve students using or creating graphic representations in their mathematics classrooms. The first section, *Reading Graphics*, shows students dealing with technical usage as they read graphs, charts, and diagrams. What definitions do they assign the mathematical terms that their teachers use? What visual model does the word conjure up for them? How can working with graphic representations provide the teacher with insight into a student's thought processes so that what Pimm (1987) calls "semantic contamination" can be identified and addressed?

The second section, *Artful Listening in Mathematics*, confronts the issue of mathematics' technical syntax. Here, students are drawing to learn. They are not copying exemplars into their notebooks for later reference but rather creating personal images of what they understand. How does syntactical subtlety lead them astray? How can the drawings that they create be a window on their thinking, especially for students who cannot adequately articulate where their confusion lies?

Regardless of whether students are reading graphic models or creating them, the teacher's questions play a key role. In addition to providing feedback about student understanding, questions also serve a mediating function, helping students discover what they know (or don't know) as they attempt to construct mathematical meaning.

In my role as a classroom-based staff developer, I observe middle school students and collect data for their teachers. After each of the lessons described in this chapter, I met with the teacher to reflect collaboratively on what I had noticed. The major reflection questions that we discussed are included at the end of each case. In some situations, based on our knowledge of particular students, we were able to tentatively solve problems through conversation. In all of the scenarios, the teachers and I looked for language-dependent impediments to learning and asked questions about how students visualized and conceptualized mathematics. These conversations heightened our appreciation of how models, metaphors, and subtle phrasing can affect visual imagery and concept formation.

# Reading Graphics: Mixed Metaphors and Double-Edged Words

*Getting the picture does not mean writing the formula or crunching the numbers, it means grasping the metaphor.* —James Bullock (1994, p. 737)

As teachers, we are advised to activate students' prior knowledge. But what if a student's knowledge is faulty or incomplete, or compromised by logical inconsistencies and faulty inferences? Barnett-Clarke (2004) calls these inconsistencies and inferences "pitfalls" and describes them as "prevalent misconceptions or inaccuracies that have logical and intuitive roots and are resistant to change. . . . These inconsistencies are often so much a part of everyday use that adults often don't realize the potential pitfalls that lurk in how students interpret what is being said or written" (p. 64). Graphic representations can invite these types of pitfalls for students, who after all are consummate literalists ("pizza wedges *are* fractions; ergo, fractions *are* pizza wedges").

In the following two scenarios, students used visual representations suggested by their teachers. Whereas the model used in the first scenario seemed new to the students, the one in the second scenario was firmly in place, having most likely been developed over several years of classroom exposure.

## Scenario #1: Measuring Cups Activity

In this 6th grade activity, students were asked to quadruple a cookie recipe. Although some ingredients could easily be scaled up (e.g., one egg would become four eggs), other ingredients were given in fractional or mixed number amounts (e.g., 1¼ cups of flour). At this point in the year, the students had not been taught a formal algorithm for adding fractions. Prior to the activity, they had been working with fraction strips (a linear model) and pictures of square pans in which "brownies" were cut into fractional pieces (an area model). The recipe, however, used a volume model based on standard measuring cups. Would the students be able to transfer understanding based on one- and two-dimensional models to this new three-dimensional situation?

For some students, the transition was not simple. When one pair had trouble finding an entry point into the problem, the teacher suggested that they draw a picture. She drew a large measuring cup, which she labeled "1 cup" and a smaller one beside it labeled "¼ cup." When the teacher left their desks, the students discussed how they might quadruple the cups and then set to work drawing their picture. I visited them when they had finished and asked about their sketch, shown in Figure 4.1.

When I asked the students how many cups of flour they would need for the larger recipe, they replied, "Eight."

Is there a logical and intuitive root to this solution? Visualize for a moment a juice glass and an iced-tea tumbler sitting next to one another on a table. How many glasses do you see? Two—one small, one large. How many cups did the students draw on their paper? Eight—four small, four large.

Questions for reflection:

• In what other ways might the students have attempted to model the problem if the teacher hadn't offered her initial suggestion?

• How might using *actual* three-dimensional models (i.e., a set of nested measuring cups) before using two-dimensional *representations* alter the transfer of learning?

• What does this encounter indicate about how students understand *quantity* (of flour in the cups) and *number* (of separate cups)? How might this understanding affect their grasp of fractions?

• How can teachers help students move fluidly between visual models so that they begin to perceive mathematical generalities?

| FIGURE 4.1 | Measuring Cups Activity Sketch for Scenario #1 |

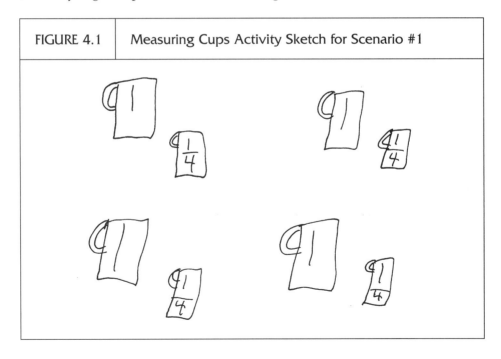

## Scenario #2: A Round Pizza in a Square Whole

"The cafeteria cook baked a pizza in a large rectangular sheet pan and put it into the school's refrigerator. That night, a hungry thief came by and ate half the pizza. The next six nights he returned, always eating half of what was left. After a week, what fraction of the pizza remained?" (Adapted from Lappan, 1998, p. 46).

In the class I was observing, the teacher set out various types and sizes of paper for students to use in modeling a solution to this problem: grid paper, construction paper, large sheets of newsprint. Some students drew lines halfway down a sheet of paper and then began subdividing it with more lines. Others folded and refolded the paper several times. Some used scissors to cut it into a sequence of progressively smaller halves.

Not William. Although he had probably eaten school-baked pizza (which is invariably served in rectangles) every Friday since kindergarten, he took a piece of paper and drew a large circle on it. For William, pizzas that were cut into fractional parts *had* to be round. He was adamant about this, even when the teacher showed him that the problem described a rectangular pan.

Questions for reflection:

• What does this encounter suggest about William's understanding of fractions?

• How might language be used to bridge what William has experienced in the cafeteria and what he has internalized from past experiences in mathematics class?

• How can the teacher help William move beyond a single conceptual image and experiment with new metaphors and visual models?

• When are models useful, and when do they get in the way of new learning?

In the next two scenarios, students mapped their prior knowledge onto a given graphic, not realizing that their personal experience was not aligned with the model. In the first scenario, a student equated a word from his informal mathematics vocabulary with formal mathematical terminology; in the second scenario, students used the everyday meaning of a phrase rather than the mathematical one.

## Scenario #3: An Uphill Struggle (Slow on a Slippery Slope)

Avery was working at the whiteboard, talking about a graph he had created. He had plotted points on a coordinate grid to indicate how fast a cyclist,

Theo, was going at various times during a trip (see Figure 4.2); for example, if the rider were traveling at a speed of 15 miles per hour at the 10-minute mark, Avery would indicate this by plotting the point (10, 15).

When the teacher asked questions relating to specific points on the graph, Avery was able to respond, but he became confused when the teacher asked if the cyclist's speed had increased or decreased between two particular points. Although the teacher had emphasized in previous lessons that points need not be connected unless there is constant change, she decided to join two points, (0, 0) and (10, 15), to help Avery visualize what happened during that interval.

To the teacher's eyes, the line she had drawn had a steep slope, indicating that Theo had increased his speed from 0 miles per hour to a brisk 15 miles per hour in the first 10 minutes of the ride. Avery didn't see it that way. He looked at the line the teacher had drawn, tensed up, and became even more confused. "He kind of slows down," he said, before changing his mind: "No! He's both increasing *and* decreasing."

| FIGURE 4.2 | Avery's Cyclist Speed Chart for Scenario #3 |
| --- | --- |

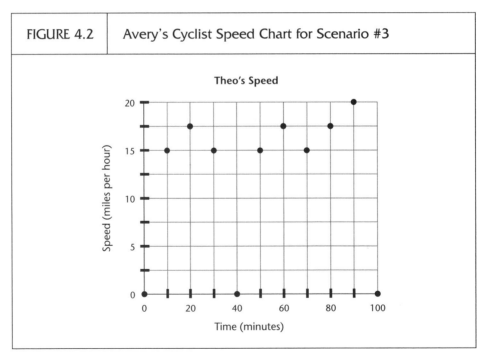

*Source:* From *Connected Mathematics: Variables & Patterns* (p. 24) © 2004 by Michigan State University, Glenda Lappan, James T. Fey, William F. Fitzgerald, Susan N. Friel, and Elizabeth D. Phillips. Published by Pearson Education, Inc., publishing as Prentice Hall. Used by permission.

The teacher continued to probe to better understand what Avery was thinking, asking him about the 30- and 50-minute marks, where the cyclist's speed was also 15 miles per hour. Avery ran his hand across the line, saying, "Well, here it's kind of leveled off. It's flat." Upon hearing this, the teacher realized that Avery saw the graph not as a representation of the cyclist's speed, but as a model of the physical terrain. Whereas for the teacher the steep slope indicated a fast increase in speed, for Avery it literally represented a hill, where hard pedaling is required and speed would most certainly decrease. Avery's misconception is not unusual: He took the phrase "a graph is a picture" quite literally to mean a picture of hills and valleys.

As teachers, we try to build on our students' novice or intuitive vocabulary, using it as a bridge to more precise terminology. Some students understand that their use of informal terms during a mathematical discussion is simply a convenient conversational substitute, lacking the precision of a more formal mathematical term (Herbel-Eisenmann, 2002). Others, however, equate terms such as *steepness* and *slope*, assuming that the two are mathematically synonymous.

Questions for reflection:

• How might a student interpret steepness if the same data were plotted on two graphs, with different intervals on their axes?

• What are the clues that a student's misunderstanding may be language-dependent?

• For how long, and to what depth, should a teacher continue to probe in order to get to the logical and intuitive root of confusion?

• To what extent should student-generated terminology be encouraged in mathematical discussions?

• At what point does such student-generated terminology inhibit rather than foster understanding?

## Scenario #4: Breaking Even

In common parlance, the word *even* suggests neatness and tidiness—an even hemline is the same length all around. The concept of even numbers might evoke images of animals entering Noah's Ark two by two. But what does the term *breaking even* mean?

In a 7th grade class, students were asked to interpret the line graph in Figure 4.3, which shows a bike shop's monthly profit or loss during the course of a year. The line zigs and zags; some months it lands above the *x*-axis, some months it settles below it, with the point for September right on the *x*-axis itself. For the months of April and May, profits are the same—$800. The

| FIGURE 4.3 | Repair Shop Profit Chart for Scenario #4 |
|---|---|

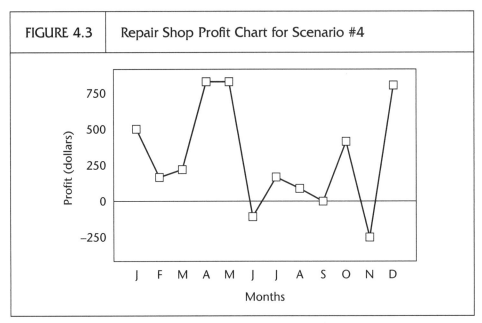

*Source:* From *Connected Mathematics: Accentuate the Negative* (p. 148) © 2002 by Michigan State University, Glenda Lappan, James T. Fey, William F. Fitzgerald, Susan N. Friel, and Elizabeth D. Phillips. Published by Pearson Education, Inc., publishing as Prentice Hall. Used by permission.

question is, in which months did the shop make money, lose money, or break even?

Several students were convinced that because the line connecting the points for April and May was "flat" (i.e., parallel to the *x*-axis), these must be the break-even months. The points for April and May were equidistant from the *x*-axis, just as my "even" hemline would be equidistant from the floor. Once the teacher became aware that the students' confusion about the phrase *breaking even* was causing an error, it was easy for him to explain it as the point at which income and expenses offset each other. Note that the phrase *breaking even* is not a formal mathematical term but rather a conversational idiom with mathematical implications. Pimm (1987) calls these types of phrases *locutions*—"certain whole expressions whose meanings cannot necessarily be understood merely by knowing the meanings of the individual words; that is, the expressions function as semantic units on their own" (p. 88).

Questions for reflection:

• Did the students understand the phrase, "where income and expenses offset each other"?

• Did the teacher's explanation seem clear to me simply because I understood it from my vantage point as an adult?

- Was there another double-edged word or convoluted metaphor hidden in the teacher's explanation that neither of us noticed, but that may surface at some other point?
- How can teachers become more aware of the mathematical locutions embedded in their classroom conversations? For example, consider the many financial, scientific, and statistical idioms used frequently when analyzing data.

The following scenarios explore the role of classroom climate in drawing meaning from graphic representations. The first scenario addresses student-to-teacher communication, whereas the second listens in on students talking to each other.

## Scenario #5: Envisioning the Invisible

One group of 6th grade students I observed had just finished a unit on fractional concepts. Before their teacher introduced them to formal operations with fractions, she had them work in a probability module that required the use of fractional notation, equivalent fractions, and the informal addition of fractions. On this particular occasion, the students were using a spinner similar to the one shown in Figure 4.4, portioned into wedges of three different designs.

A single one-sixth portion of the spinner has stripes; two noncontiguous sixths have dots. The remaining sixths have hearts on them: a one-sixth slice on the right side of the spinner and a one-third wedge on the left. The students' task was twofold: First they needed to spin the spinner 30 times and report, in fractional form, the results of landing on each design. Second, they were to analyze the spinner, by measuring it with an angle ruler or by some other method, to determine the fractional portion of stripes, dots, and hearts.

Most of the students opted not to use the angle ruler. Some cut out the spinner, creased it across the middle,

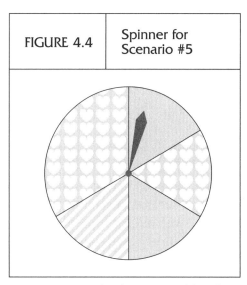

| FIGURE 4.4 | Spinner for Scenario #5 |

*Source:* From *Connected Mathematics: How Likely Is It?* (p. 24) © 2004 by Michigan State University, Glenda Lappan, James T. Fey, William F. Fitzgerald, Susan N. Friel, and Elizabeth D. Phillips. Published by Pearson Education, Inc., publishing as Prentice Hall. Used by permission.

and then folded the resulting semi-circle into thirds using the one-sixth markings as a guide. Others cut the spinner apart and repositioned the pieces so that those with the same design were adjacent to each other. Still other students drew what they termed "invisible lines" dividing the one-third chunk in half so that the spinner was composed of six one-sixth sections.

The class discussion that followed this activity was lively. Students shared their strategies, argued as to whether or not the sections with the same design must be adjacent, suggested which designs one should "bet on" to win, noted how a "50-50 chance" really meant a 50 *percent* chance, and discussed the differences between their experimental results and what each fractional portion of the spinner predicted. It looked as if the class had a solid understanding of the concepts.

As the discussion wound down, Sonya spoke for the first time. Pointing to the line splitting the one-third wedge in two, she asked, "Will they still be sixths if the invisible line isn't there?"

Questions for reflection:

• Did Sonya's question indicate confusion about equivalent fractions? Or was she trying to clarify a precise perception of the visual image?

• What understanding did Sonya have about the concepts her classmates had just discussed?

• Could Sonya have asked her question earlier? Or did her classmates' vigorous discussion help her formulate her question?

• What classroom dynamics were in place that allowed Sonya to feel comfortable asking such a basic question?

## Scenario #6: The Wordsmiths

Students often know that *something* is happening in a table or graph, that a pattern is right *there*. They see it clearly, but. . . . It's frustrating for any of us to grope for words.

In an 8th grade class that was starting a unit on exponential decay, the students were visibly engaged as they pointed at numbers on the table of values they had created. Their hands were flailing, they were rolling their eyes upward, searching for a word somewhere in the back of their minds and, when not finding one, inventing terms as they tried to express what they wanted to communicate. In short, they acted precisely the way travelers abroad do when forced to communicate in a language not their own.

Lacking precise terminology, these students began to describe what they saw happening on their table of values by relating decay to exponential growth. If things grew exponentially by doubling in yesterday's lesson on exponential growth, then today things seemed to be getting smaller by "undoubling." Or maybe it is called "doubling down." It certainly would work if you "divided it in half." Would that be the same as "taking half of it"? Or "dividing by two"? Would that be "halving"? Is that "the opposite of doubling"? Nothing was said about reciprocals or inverse operations . . . yet.

Questions for reflection:

• What might the teacher have done to foster a classroom climate in which students felt comfortable talking to each other about emerging mathematical ideas?

• Would this particular mathematical conversation have occurred if the students didn't have a graphic "prop"?

• How did the visual representation act as a catalyst for student discourse?

• How might conversations about a graphic display encourage students to put their mathematical perceptions into writing?

• Now that a conversation had begun on the topic of exponential decay, how might the teacher build on the richly descriptive terms that the students created to press for more precise mathematical terminology?

## Artful Listening in Mathematics: The Subtleties of Syntax

"Show and Tell" is one of the earliest ways that children learn to communicate in the classroom. Youngsters who are normally shy and inarticulate when asked to talk in front of a group start to relax when holding a prop that they can talk about. What can this primary-grade communication strategy suggest to teachers who are trying to help older students develop oral communication skills in mathematics? Moreover, how might teachers use this approach to draw out misconceptions and flaws in student thinking? The answer may be as simple as asking students to create a "prop" that they can talk about by literally drawing one out. If a teacher suspects that a student's concept image is "sketchy," wouldn't it be useful to get that image on paper? When students create visual images, they are externalizing their mathematical thought processes, even if they do not have the precise mathematical language with which to express their ideas.

In the following scenarios, students were deep in the process of constructing mathematical meaning. However, unlike the students in the preceding section, who often seemed frustrated or confused, these students were confident that they had listened to their teachers and understood what had been said. All these students, however, missed crucial nuances in their teachers' mathematical syntax and unfortunately began to build conceptual misunderstandings based on faulty assumptions. Because these students had a less-developed mathematical grammar and syntax, they struggled to translate their mathematical ideas into words.

Students are often asked to look at a mathematical diagram and interpret it orally. In the following scenarios, the students did the opposite: having listened to mathematical words, they created interpretive sketches. As you read these scenarios, try to visualize the students' drawings as you consider the following questions:

- What did the teacher mean?
- What did the teacher say?
- What did the student hear?
- What visual image did the student create to match what he or she heard?

## Scenario #7: Where's the Fourth Fourth?

Rather than introduce fractional concepts using her own visual models, one 6th grade teacher routinely encouraged her students to draw what *they* thought she had said about fractions during a lesson. In this fraction module's first activity, students were given 1" × 8½" strips of blank paper that they attempted to fold into halves, thirds, fourths, fifths, sixths, eighths, ninths, tenths, and twelfths. The class worked with their fraction strips for several days, naming them, comparing them, finding fractions that were equivalent to each other, and, finally, labeling the strips in symbolic *a/b* form. One student, Benjamin, showed me his fraction strip for fourths. It was precisely labeled on each of its three folds: ¼, ²⁄₄, ¾ (see Figure 4.5).

When I asked him, Benjamin told me that this strip represented thirds: "The whole thing is divided into three parts." When I asked about some of the other strips, each of which was correctly labeled, Benjamin followed the same line of thinking: his name for the strip was based on the last numerator in the series. When I asked him about the strip that was folded in half, he seemed confused. Intuitively, he knew that he should call it a "halves" strip, but the numerator was a "1." The system he had carefully constructed didn't work in this particular case. How can that be?

| FIGURE 4.5 | Benjamin's Fraction Strips for Scenario #7 |
| --- | --- |

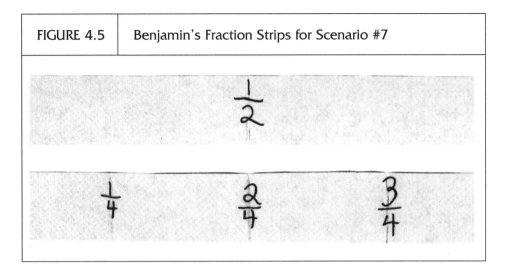

Questions for reflection:

• What distinction was Benjamin making between the terms *thirds, three folds,* and *dividing into three parts*?

• How might students conceptualize *fourths* differently, depending on whether they are asked to label the strip's *segments* ($\frac{1}{4}$, $\frac{2}{4}$, $\frac{3}{4}$, $\frac{4}{4}$) or its *folds* ($\frac{1}{4}$, $\frac{2}{4}$, $\frac{3}{4}$)?

• What consideration might the teacher need to give to precision of language when providing directions for this task?

• What role might peer-to-peer discourse have played in helping Benjamin test his conjecture?

• What questions might a teacher ask to check more deeply for understanding if, at first glance, a student's thoughtfully done work is apparently correct?

## Scenario #8: Three Three/Ten Combos

Later in the same module, Benjamin's class was introduced to area models for fractions. The first activity for this unit had students divide pictures of square baking pans into 15 equal-sized brownies. Although a few students "cut" the pan into thin, biscotti-like brownies (a $1 \times 15$ arrangement), most drew lines creating a $3 \times 5$ grid. When asked to cut the brownies into 30ths, all but one student decided that 30 ultra-thin biscotti ($1 \times 30$) were too tiresome and imprecise to draw. The most popular arrangements were $5 \times 6$, $3 \times 10$, and $2 \times 15$ (the $1 \times 15$ biscotti cut crosswise into halves).

This model of vertical and horizontal cuts became familiar to the students after several days. Benjamin was building on this understanding of area models for fractions when he started to work with decimals. After an initial activity in which the students planned a garden using a hundredths grid, the teacher distributed a paper on which there was a large square divided vertically into tenths. When asked to model three-tenths, Benjamin immediately took up his pencil and divided the square crosswise into thirds, creating 30 equal parts as shown in Figure 4.6.

When questioned about his approach, Benjamin responded, "This is three"—indicating his horizontal cuts—"and tenths"—indicating the vertical lines printed on the template.

Questions for reflection:

- From what assumptions might Benjamin have been working when he approached this new concept?

| FIGURE 4.6 | Benjamin's Tenths Grid for Scenario #8 |
| --- | --- |

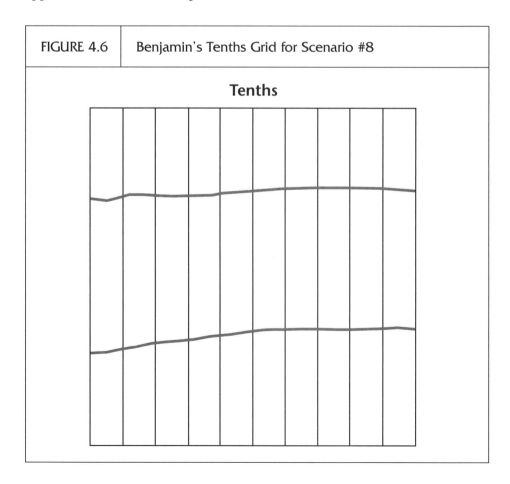

**Tenths**

- Where was there a language-based component in his confusion?
- What do the phrases "three-tenths," "three and tenths," and "thirds and tenths" mean mathematically? What do they seem to mean to Benjamin?
- In a roomful of 20 students, how difficult is it to hear the subtleties of different word forms?
- What might Benjamin's drawing imply about what he heard?
- How could the teacher use Benjamin's drawing to encourage him to express his personal understanding in words?
- How might making additional sketches have helped Benjamin communicate what he heard and understood?

## Scenario #9: Holes in Her Logic

Sarah's 6th grade class was finishing a unit on fraction-decimal equivalents. On this particular day, the teacher gave the students a list of foods donated to a hurricane relief project and asked them to determine how the food could be equally distributed among 24 families.

Sarah began by drawing 24 squares to represent a box for each family. For 48 cans of cocoa, she counted aloud as she put one dot representing one can into each box. She repeated this procedure once more so that each square contained two dots. Then she erased the dots. She used the same strategy for the 72 boxes of powdered milk. When she got to the 264 juice boxes, however, she switched to a calculator. She entered the division problem correctly and wrote the result, 11, on her answer sheet. When faced with the task of dividing up 12 pounds of cheddar cheese, Sarah again reached for her calculator and pressed the correct keys: 12, ÷, 24, =. Rather than writing the answer on her worksheet, she reached for the sheet of box diagrams and began putting little circles in each of the 24 boxes, as shown in Figure 4.7.

What was Sarah doing? Had she forgotten to record her answer and moved instead to the next question, which involved dividing up six pounds of *Swiss* cheese? Is that what she was drawing?

Sarah seemed proud and confident when she explained her work to me. I asked her where the five dots that she had put into each box had come from. Why, she had read that right off her calculator screen: they were "point-five."

Questions for reflection:

- What windows to Sarah's thinking do her cocoa, milk, and cheese drawings provide?
- How did Sarah seem to understand division in general? What about division in situations in which the quotient is greater than one? When the quotient is less than one?

| FIGURE 4.7 | Box Diagrams for Scenario #9 |
|---|---|

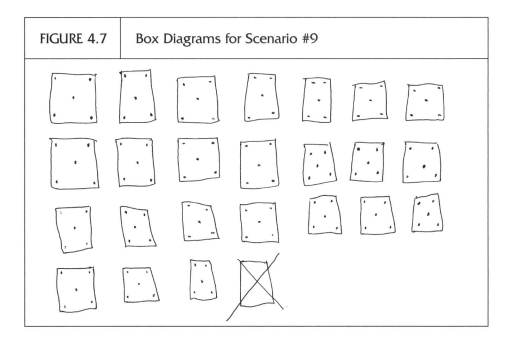

- What did Sarah believe about the decimal point?
- What was Sarah hearing, and how did this influence the manner in which she conceptualized decimal fractions?
- What is appropriate calculator use for students beginning to work with fractions and decimals?
- Would language-based cues, such as the teacher's asking how to divide a 12-pound *wheel* (or *chunk*) of cheese among 24 families, suggest useful visual models? Or might metaphors create further confusion?
- What might the teacher do to reinforce the use of proper terminology when students are working with decimal fractions?

## Scenario #10: What Does *More* Mean?

One way that teachers can use language to help students make sense of mathematics is to contextualize problems by "wrapping words around the numbers." The words, in turn, may give rise to images that students can use when formulating solutions. However, paragraph-sized narratives present problems of their own. Often numbers are written as words rather than as numerals (e.g., "five" rather than "5"). There might be extraneous information that needs to be disregarded. Or maybe the question that students need to answer is at the end of the paragraph, and they've forgotten the details they've just read. It is always useful for teachers to assume their students' mind-set and attempt problems from their perspective. What phrases do you think you'd want clarified? What language would you need to have "debugged"?

Consider the following problem adapted from "Comparing and Scaling," a 7th grade *Connected Mathematics* module on proportional thinking (Lappan, 2002b). It may help you to visualize the problem if you pick up a pencil and make a drawing of your own.

> You and 17 colleagues are meeting for dinner at Nona's Italian Restaurant before a parent open house. Because you want to socialize as a group, you prefer not to sit at one long banquet table, nor do you want to be split up among many small tables. The manager accommodates by pushing together three small tables to create seating for eight, and four small tables to create seating for ten. When dinner is served, one pizza is placed on each of these small tables: three for the group of eight, four for the group of ten. In each group the pizza is shared equally among tablemates. Would you get the same amount of pizza regardless of where you sat? If the amounts were different, at which table would you get more? Explain your reasoning. (p. 30)

Before reading the classroom description, ask yourself the following questions:
- As written in the students' textbooks, the problem has pizza being served at cafeteria tables. In the revised version above, the problem is situated in an adult context. Did the restaurant context help you develop a mental image of the mathematics involved?
- Did you create a sketch when solving the problem? If you didn't, why not? If you did, was it helpful in solving the problem? Were your eyes drawn back to read the text as your hand created the visual image? Did drawing help you clarify what you had read? Did your experience in sketching to solve the problem mirror the opinion of Reehm and Long (1996)—namely, that drawing helps us "to perform the indicated computations, answer questions, or draw appropriate graphs or diagrams . . . [and] is essential for comprehension" (p. 38)?

The lesson I observed started with the teacher's referring back to prior work with rates, ratios, and proportions. After receiving student feedback about these topics, the teacher read the day's problem to the class and showed them a transparency of the seating arrangement. Armand's 7th grade textbook also had a diagram of the problem's seating arrangement, and he began by copying it. Working alone, he sketched two rectangles to designate tables but did not draw anything to indicate seats or people around them. He continued by drawing circles on each rectangle to represent the appropriate number of pizzas. He then sectioned each circle into either eight or ten wedges, depending on how many people were to be seated at each table. (Creating tenths was bothersome and involved multiple erasures.) Then he stopped. Other students continued to work, setting up proportions, changing $\frac{4}{10}$ to the equivalent fraction $\frac{2}{5}$, and finding the decimal equivalents for $\frac{4}{10}$ and $\frac{3}{8}$.

Armand's hand was the first one up when the time came for students to report their findings. He used his diagram to show that each person at the table of eight will get three pieces of pizza, while each person at the table of 10 will get four pieces. He reasoned that a person will get more at the table of 10 because, "You get more pieces." The teacher pressed for further explanation:

**Teacher:** But I'm not asking you how many *pieces*. How do you know it's more pizza?

**Armand:** Well, I cut each pizza in 10.

**Teacher:** But what about the size of each piece of pizza?

**Armand:** I have one piece from each pizza for each person.

**Teacher:** But why is that more pizza?

**Armand:** Because it's four pieces each.

**Teacher:** But why is that more *pizza*?

**Armand:** Because it's *four!*

Questions for reflection:

• Compare the use of the singular noun *pizza* in these two sentences from the problem. How is the meaning of the word *pizza* different in each instance?

   – "Each pizza is cut into eight slices."

   – "In each group the pizza is shared equally."

• Read the following paragraph; then think about how the word *more* is used in everyday conversation and how it is used in a mathematical context:

> The distinction between *count nouns* and *mass nouns* . . . is the distinction between discrete and continuous quantity. When we talk of discrete quantity, we use *count nouns* and we may have <u>many</u> or <u>few</u> of them. On the other hand, when we talk of continuous quantity, we use *mass nouns*, and we may have <u>much</u> or <u>little</u> of the referent entity. In comparing discrete quantities we talk about <u>more</u> and <u>fewer</u>, while in comparing continuous quantities we use <u>more</u> and <u>less</u>. (Schwartz, 1996, p. 8)

• Refer back to the text of the Nona's Restaurant problem, and analyze it for instances of discrete versus continuous quantity. Where do you note a shift from one concept to the other?

- How might the teacher explain to Armand the distinction between "how much pizza" and "how many pieces"?
- How could the teacher use language in conjunction with Armand's drawing to help him reframe the problem?
- At the quick-checkout register of your supermarket, does the sign say "Ten Items or Less" or "Ten Items or Fewer"? What is the semantic difference?

When teachers are asked in post-observation conferences to reflect on how student drawings can inform their practice, three themes emerge. Teachers feel that the drawings

1. Make the students more aware that they're "speaking mathematics" in class,

2. Show a need for greater precision in the students' use of mathematical language, and

3. Suggest areas in which directions and explanations should be more clearly phrased.

## Suggestions from Teachers

How can we help students understand the graphic and figurative language of what Krussel (1998) terms "the mathematical community's existing body of metaphors" (p. 49)? Many suggestions emerged during my conversations with teachers:

- Combine the verbal with the visual. When dealing with words that have ambiguous meanings, consider having students fill in graphic organizers or concept maps.
- Monitor your use of metaphors, models, and idioms. Experienced middle school teachers routinely monitor their vocabulary in order to avoid using everyday words that have titillating double meanings for students. Similarly, teachers should identify terms that have both conversational and separate mathematical meanings, clarify these differences for students, and watch for any incorrect but logical and intuitive roots that hinder understanding.
- Assume positive intent. Students may couch their mathematical questions or observations in offhand, joking, or even dismissive tones. Speaking half-formed thoughts in front of their peers can be so uncomfortable that students may feel safer playing the clown than risk asking what they fear might be a foolish question. As teachers, we need to believe that in every question asked, in every answer given, there is the kernel of a student's struggle to understand and to make mathematical meaning.

• Once students are comfortable showing their understanding by drawing pictures, encourage them to move to a more stylized representation of the same concept. Moving from a detailed picture to a simplified shape, often called an *icon*, is another step toward mathematical abstraction.

• Consider the order in which individual students select different forms of representation. What sequence seems to promote depth of mathematical thinking for the specific topic being studied? What implication does this have for lesson planning?

• Actively point out connections to other mathematical representations. Clement (2004) describes a representations model shaped like a five-pointed star in which the contextual, spoken, pictorial, tactile, and written symbols are interconnected and where the goal is for students to become fluent in translating one representation into another.

To help students better visualize the language of mathematics, teachers suggest the following practices, which can be incorporated into classrooms with minimum disruption:

• Articulate and enunciate, being especially conscious of word endings, pronoun referents, and "little words" that tend to be murmured or mumbled.

• Buy pencils, and keep them sharpened. Sharpened no. 2 pencils and good erasers need to be classroom basics if students are expected to communicate by drawing.

• Provide enough time for students who need to draw in order to learn. The kinesthetic act of putting ideas on paper, whether by drawing or writing, takes more time than talking. It is reasonable to assume that one benefit of drawing and writing in mathematics is that it slows down our thinking.

• When assigning open-response questions that require both writing and drawing, suggest that students create the diagram first in order to have something concrete to write about.

• Make copies of key textbook pages so that students can write notes on them, add diagrams, doodle in the margins, and underline words. This allows students to engage with the text in a tactile, kinesthetic, physical way.

• Have students use a graphic organizer, preferably one that incorporates both words and images. According to one study, students who were taught how to use graphic organizers for test preparation retained significantly more information than did other students (Dickson, Simmons, & Kameenui, 1995). The Verbal and Visual Word Association (Readence, Bean, & Baldwin, 1998) is a powerful but simple graphic organizer consisting of a plain index card divided into four quadrants with places for a word or phrase (upper left), its definition (lower left), a visual representation (upper right), and a personal association (lower right).

• Designate an area for sketching when creating templates and worksheets. Students who find it useful to scribble and sketch often do so on a piece of scrap paper that gets tossed in the trash at the end of class. Allotting a section of the page for drawing indicates that you value and expect to see visual thinking.

## Mathematics: A Visual Language for All Students

Although student-generated drawings can help teachers root out mathematical misconceptions, they are much more than a diagnostic tool. For kinesthetic learners and geometric thinkers, sketching may be a preferred strategy for processing the language of mathematics into learning. For these students, drawing is not just a way to make their thoughts about mathematics visible to others; it is a device to capture the language of mathematics in order to make it visible to themselves. Even for students who approach learning through other pathways, the kinesthetic act of drawing may be valuable. Drawing slows students down and allows them to self-correct their thoughts while their hands are sketching; it also helps them to keep track of and record their solutions (Albert, 2000).

Research studies have shown that drawing helps students better understand the material. As Borasi, Siegal, Fonzi, and Smith (1998) note, "The act of recasting meanings generated in one sign system (language), into another (visual art), is intended to invite reflection from a different perspective, a move that can lead to new insights. Because no code for translating language into visual images exists prior to the creation of sketches, students must invent their own. It is this act of crossing the gap between alternative symbolic systems that gives sketching its generative potential" (p. 280).

The classroom scenarios presented in this chapter suggest that mathematical language influences the drawings students create, first in their thoughts and then on paper. But might students' visual images also influence their mathematical language? It seems probable that when drawing accompanies talking and writing, students develop both visual and verbal literacy.

# Discourse in the Mathematics Classroom

*Euthecia Hancewicz*

Students construct meaning of the mathematics they encounter through many experiences. They travel through their daily lives bumping up against mathematics without even knowing it as they play with toys and games or work with money and tools. As they progress through our mathematics classes, they adapt to a dozen or so different teachers and a variety of textbooks.

As teachers, we naturally hope our students will attain deep mathematical understanding in our classrooms. One powerful tool for enhancing that understanding is classroom discourse. The NCTM's *Principles and Standards for School Mathematics* (2000) speaks to the need for students to make conjectures, experiment with problem-solving strategies, argue about mathematics, and justify their thinking. There is general agreement that discussion and argumentation improve conceptual understanding.

For the purposes of this chapter, I am defining *discourse* as the genuine sharing of ideas among participants in a mathematics lesson, including both talking and active listening. Such sharing occurs on many levels—between teacher and student, between student and student, within small groups, and within the whole-class group. I will focus mainly on whole-class discussions, keeping in mind that stirring up an argument can lead to improved learning. Great conversations happen only when genuine discourse becomes the culture of the classroom.

## What Discourse Looks Like

As a math teacher coach, I have either observed or been a participant in countless classroom conversations, ranging from traditional teacher-centered interchanges to discourse-rich student-led discussions.

- *Traditional.* The teacher and several students talk. The teacher asks most of the questions, which are directed at specific students who in turn respond directly to the teacher. There are brief conversations between the teacher and individuals. Other students are expected to listen. When a student doesn't respond to a question as the teacher expects, prompts from the teacher generally lead to a preplanned answer.
- *Probing.* The teacher is still the leader, and conversations are still between the teacher and individual students, but questions are more open. They stem from the teacher's desire to hear about students' thinking, rather than from a need to move students along a planned route—from a desire to elicit ideas for further thinking and to pique the interest of other students. Common questions in this type of interchange include, "How does that fit with what [another student] said?" and "How did you decide to do what you did?"
- *Discourse-Rich.* Young people work toward mathematical understanding by sharing ideas with each other and the teacher. As Stigler and Hiebert (1999) note, "Students must . . . learn to question and probe one another's thinking in order to clarify underdeveloped ideas" (pp. 90–91). When this type of conversation becomes the culture of a classroom, students uncover new ways to conceptualize mathematics.

One day, Ariel, a student in Mr. Ryan's 7th grade class, was explaining his method of estimating the distance around a trapezoid drawn on unit grid paper so that $AB$ = one unit (see Figure 5.1). "I counted the units and the perimeter is five units," he said, demonstrating on the projected image of the shape by counting $BC$ as two units and each of the other sides, $AB$, $AD$, and $DC$, as one unit.

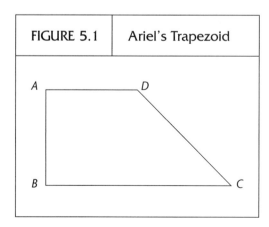

FIGURE 5.1    Ariel's Trapezoid

Belinda's hand shot up. "I think it's more than five units," she said. Several other student looked perplexed, so Mr. Ryan gave the class one of his well-known "I wonder" looks. Ariel was at the whiteboard, so he explained his thinking again, but Belinda wasn't convinced. "Then you come up and do it!" said Ariel.

At this point, Mr. Ryan walked to the back of the classroom and sat at an empty student desk.

Belinda said she thought the segment *CD* was longer than one unit because it was tipped. There was some general chatter among the classmates; then Charlie said, "I agree, and I can prove it." He took a ruler to the front of the classroom, laid it along the *AB* segment and put a finger at the spot where one unit hit the ruler. The class attentively listened as he explained, "I call this one unit even though it isn't matching one inch on the ruler." Then he laid the ruler along the *DC* segment, thinking he'd show that it was longer than one unit.

His classmates weren't satisfied. Several accused him of making up the unit and moving his finger.

Now Dara jumped up. "I can prove it!" she said. Her method involved marking the length of the *AB* segment on a piece of paper and comparing that to the length of the *DC* line. Her demonstration convinced the class that the *DC* line was longer than *AB,* so the perimeter had to exceed five units.

Mr. Ryan returned to his role as leader, happy to have let the students conduct this investigation on their own.

When the classroom climate fosters genuine student discourse, students react to their classmates' ideas, asking questions and checking for understanding. Conversations continue without the need for teacher participation or supervision.

## Creating Discourse-Friendly Classrooms

Moving from traditional student-teacher interchanges to rich classroom discourse is not an easy or superficial change; it requires a major shift in one's definition of effective teaching. If we believe that the goal of teaching is for students to become proficient at a set of procedures, then it is logical to craft lessons that help them move gradually along a planned sequence of increasingly more sophisticated procedures. However, if we believe that the goal is for students to build mathematical understanding as well as efficient procedures, a well-crafted lesson depends upon the students effectively sharing their strategies and ideas. Thoughtful teachers use student ideas as springboards for powerful lessons. Discourse is more than a teaching technique; it is a framework on which to build effective mathematics lessons.

In an article entitled "Talking Their Way to the Middle of All Numbers," Kristine Woleck (2001) gives us a view of how she used student conversations to build a 1st grade lesson about infinity. In the midst of a conversation about temperatures, one of Woleck's students commented that 25 degrees was "halfway between 20 and 30! It's in the middle." Another student's response to this observation was, "I'm wondering, what is the middle of all numbers?" Woleck goes on to tell us how she was able to let this kernel of an idea grow into an exploration of the abstract concept of infinity. The discussion was accessible and meaningful to all the students regardless of their level of mathematical understanding. Student voices give a sense of the flow of their ideas:

> **Ryan:** "Fifty is the middle, because 50 plus 50 equals 100."
>
> **Elizabeth:** "But you can count to more than 100."
>
> **Antoine:** "There's no middle number because numbers never stop."
>
> **Whitney:** "If you count to an even number, then there will be two numbers in the middle. If it's an odd number, then there's one number in the middle."
>
> **Kevin:** "The problem is numbers never stop."
>
> **Whitney:** "Well, the numbers go so far up, but what's the biggest negative number?"

Woleck had created a classroom environment in which students shared their ideas and challenged each other under her guidance. As she notes in her article, her "ears were open that day" and she was able to let the student voices lead an exploration of one of mathematics' big ideas (p. 30).

As I coach teachers, I help them plan lessons, I observe the lessons, and I follow up with reflective conversations. I've been part of teachers' lives as they work to shift from traditional teacher-centered classrooms to discourse-rich ones. This difficult switch requires a whole new belief about what learning is. I am convinced that small changes can help teachers move forward without a major upheaval. The following is a list of personal suggestions for small but significant changes teachers can make:

• Arrange furniture so that students can easily turn to see each other. They must be able to speak and listen to classmates.

• Encourage students to direct questions and explanations to the class, rather than to the teacher.

• When recording ideas on chalkboard or chart paper, use the students' words as much as possible. This is a matter of respecting their ideas.

• Try not to repeat or paraphrase everything students say. Paraphrasing can give the impression that the student is being corrected and may indicate to others that they don't need to listen unless the teacher speaks.

• Remind students that conversation is a two-way operation requiring both talking and listening.

- Stand in a variety of spots. As students turn to look at you, their views of the classroom and their positions relative to classmates will shift.
- Remember, students listen harder when a peer speaks than when an adult does!
- Give students time to think. Wait time or brief writing moments help students to solidify ideas and formulate good questions.
- Arrange lessons so that students have a product to share as they explain their thinking. They might illustrate ideas on chart paper or overhead transparencies or demonstrate by using manipulative materials.

Another strategy is to use favorite activities to foster discourse. In her book *Teaching Mathematics Vocabulary in Context* (2004), Miki Murray provides directions for the game, "I Have, Who Has?" and explains how her class expanded on it (Figure 5.2 shows a sample set of cards for use in the game):

> The game (exercise, really) goes like this: The cards are randomly distributed among students. Everyone gets at least one card, but many students will have more than one. A student is selected at random to go first. She selects one of her cards, ignores the "I have" at the top, and carefully reads the "Who has" definition. Students must focus and listen carefully to decide whether the definition matches one of their words. The person who has the word being defined calls out "I have" followed by the word. That person then reads the "Who has" definition on her card. The game continues until all the definitions have been read. The cards are designed so that the student who began the game will have the final word at the top of the beginning card. (p. 63)

The love Murray's students had for this activity led them to create a version using their own terms and definitions. This led to all sorts of student conversations: brainstorming words to use, figuring out the criteria for high-quality definitions, peer critiques, and testing the game.

As teachers shift toward increasingly discourse-friendly classrooms, we must cede some control. Managing conversations among students about their emerging knowledge allows discussions to move beyond the planned lesson. Teachers must understand mathematics at a deep level in order to follow young people's unconventional reasoning. We must understand the concepts that provide the foundation for each day's learning, recognize how today's lesson builds toward future concepts, be clear about connections across strands,

| FIGURE 5.2 | Sample Cards for the "I Have, Who Has?" Game |
|------------|-----------------------------------------------|

| I have **RIGHT ANGLE** Who has a five-sided polygon? | I have **ACUTE TRIANGLE** Who has a rectangle with four congruent sides? | I have **RHOMBUS** Who has a quadrilateral with only two parallel sides? |
|---|---|---|
| I have **PENTAGON** Who has the value of pi to the hundredths place? | I have **SQUARE** Who has a polygon with six sides? | I have **TRAPEZOID** Who has a chord of a circle which goes through the center? |
| I have **3.14** Who has an eight-sided polygon? | I have **HEXAGON** Who has lines in a plane that never intersect? | I have **DIAMETER** Who has a nine-sided figure? |
| I have **OCTAGON** Who has the instrument used to construct circles? | I have **PARALLEL LINES** Who has an angle with exactly 180 degrees? | I have **NONAGON** Who has figures with exactly the same shape and same size? |
| I have **COMPASS** Who has the type of triangle with all angles less than 90 degrees? | I have **STRAIGHT ANGLE** Who has a parallelogram with all sides congruent? | I have **CONGRUENT** Who has an angle with exactly 90 degrees? |

*Source:* Adapted from "I Have, Who Has?" by the Association of Teachers of Mathematics in Maine, Winter 2000, *ATOMIM Newsletter*, p. 11. Copyright © 2000 by the Association of Teachers of Mathematics in Maine. Used with permission.

and keep sight of the overarching ideas of mathematics. As Woleck (2001) reminds us, "the 'big ideas' of mathematics develop at different rates for each learner. . . . Children will revisit and refine their understanding" (p. 31).

Thoughtful participation in discourse with students informs teachers as they make instructional decisions. Here are several ways to let student ideas take the lead in class:

• Involve students in engaging and challenging problems.

• Ask open questions to stimulate student thinking. (Examples: "What does this make you wonder about?" "Are there patterns?" "Is this logical?" "Can we estimate a solution?")

• Listen carefully to student responses. Ask for clarification so that you and others really understand. Diagrams, physical models, and nonmathematical vocabulary may help students explain.

• Train students to listen to their classmates' observations by asking questions that engage: "Does this work?" "What do others suggest?" In one classroom, the teacher routinely used a single word to stimulate. He would simply say, "More?" and students would add their ideas to the interchange. He would repeat the word several times with no further comment until no one had anything else to offer. Students would then discuss the lesson, uncovering and sorting its key concepts.

• Honor diverse ideas, methods, and examples from varied sources. Students may explain most clearly by using pictures, computer illustrations, and stories.

• Honor ideas even if they're incorrect. Do not quickly agree or disagree. Students will come to realize that you are giving them time to think and to justify. Often, as students explain erroneous thinking, they uncover their own errors or classmates step in to clarify or correct them.

• Encourage mathematical arguments between students. Kids love it! The whole class benefits when students follow along as a few classmates argue their way through mathematical misunderstandings.

• Remember, confusion is okay. Years ago, my insightful mentor called it "disequilibrium." Some of the best learning happens when we sort out what it is that has pushed us a bit out of balance. Be sure students know you are deliberately letting them be confused and that this is based upon your knowledge of how people learn, as this tactic may not match what previous teachers have done.

• Take time to let students share different problem-solving methods. Even when a correct solution has been shown, ask if there are other ways to do the problem. This helps to deepen understanding and makes students more willing to work with their own strategies, rather than thinking there is only one correct method.

• Tangents are good. If an idea emerges from class discourse and captures the group's imagination, go with it. Keep the big ideas in mind, and don't forget to return to the concepts you plan to teach, but capture those teachable moments.

A few years ago, my 8th grade class and I were examining the area of parallelograms. My students were having a very hard time moving to the generalization that an area could be calculated by multiplying the base length by the height (and not by the side length). One student tried to show us her understanding by drawing a rectangle with "hinged" corners. Her drawing was confusing, so she asked if we could make some "hinged" rectangles. Another student suggested that we could make all kinds of shapes with "hinged" corners. My thought was, *So much for today's lesson!*

Our detour into this investigation took an extra day, with much design and construction work being done at home, but the rich mathematical understanding that evolved was noteworthy. Students really learned what happens to the area inside a polygon as side lengths remain stable while altitudes vary—and they discovered special characteristics of triangles as a bonus!

• Decide how much leadership your students need. I've implied that we should let students' ideas lead, but this doesn't mean that the class just moves without teacher direction. We make dozens of decisions in the course of each class period. It's up to us to ground lessons in the important ideas. Students need leadership; they need information, clarification, modeling, and support of many kinds. As we work to let student ideas lead, our skills as traditional teachers are still vitally important.

Pisauro (2002) provides some excellent instructional tips for facilitating classroom discussions. They may be summarized as follows:

• Focus student attention on a problem, puzzle, figure, process, question, or set of numbers. Stimulate discussion by asking the following types of questions:
  – What do you notice about . . . ?
  – Do you see any patterns?
  – What is similar about _____ and _____?
  – What is different about _____ and _____?
  – How do you think this works?
  – Why does this work/look this way/give this result?
  – What questions do you have?
  – What can we do with this information?
  – What do you want to know?

• As students respond, list their statements on the board where all can see. Encourage them to write the ideas in their mathematics notebooks. Rather than rephrasing their responses, ask, "How do you want to say this?"

• When observations or questions are brought up by one student, ask, "What do the rest of you think about this idea? Does it make sense?" Encourage them to consider other examples that would show that the observation is or is not always true.

• Motivate students to search for patterns, delve deeper, and generalize.

• If students are making mistakes or doing something awkwardly, ask them, "Is there an easier or more efficient way?" or "In what other ways could this be done?" rather than telling them how to do it.

• If students have difficulty thinking about a concept, suggest examples to consider or play devil's advocate. Ask "What if?" questions.

• Counter questions with questions instead of explanations. People tend to blank out when one person asks a question and the teacher immediately gives an explanation. Asking another question or saying, "What do the rest of you think about that?" tends to engage everyone's thinking.

• Even when a solution is successful, take time to ask whether anyone did the problem a different way or discarded an idea. Help students to build confidence in their own ideas, knowledge, and insights by showing that problems can be solved in a variety of ways.

## Discourse and Computation

We lament that students can't do arithmetic computation. Though we hate to spend precious time on drills and practice, we know that efficiency comes from experience. But there will be less need for drills if we foster rich discourse as we help students develop efficient algorithms. The following case illustrates the richness we can provide when we take advantage of an opportunity for real mathematical conversation.

Kerri, a 5th grade teacher, wanted her students to study two-digit multiplication. Students used base-10 blocks to figure out several products, starting with $2 \times 14$. After they did this a few times, Kerri asked them to look at the arithmetic example she wrote on the chalkboard:

$$\begin{array}{r} 14 \\ \times\ 2 \\ \hline \end{array}$$

She turned to the class and asked, "How should we start?" Several students told her to start with $2 \times 4$. Kerri asked, "Could we start with the $2 \times 1$?" Some said yes, some no. Kerri smiled and continued the discussion: "OK, tell me what to do."

The most confident voices led, using the standard algorithm they had previously learned. As Kerri recorded each step, she pointed out connections to the work students had been doing with the blocks. Because the speakers were the most "advanced" students, everyone seemed happy with their answer of 28.

Kerri smiled and then looked puzzled. She reminded the class that some students had said it was okay to start with $2 \times 1$ and asked one student to show the class how to do that. The student said, "Multiply $2 \times 1$, and write the product 2 under the 1." Kerri pushed him to explain why the 2 needed to go under the 1. He said he wasn't sure but that he knew the final answer would be 28. There were several tries at justifying, but no one pointed out that in this problem, the 2 really represents 20.

Another student, Rachel, suggested writing the 2 under the 1 and putting a 0 above the 1 in 14. "Finally, the value of 20," I thought, but nobody pointed this out. Students didn't like Rachel's method, saying it would get too complicated if the product of the ones were greater than 9. A student named Megan said she'd tried the strategy, shown in Figure 5.3, which she called the "backwards" method, with $2 \times 18$.

The class period was over. No one had produced a satisfactory explanation for why Megan's "backwards" method worked, but all the students had been thinking, had strengthened their sense of place value, and were working toward an efficient algorithm that matched their understanding. This had been a difficult discussion for some, illuminating for others. Allowing students to share their emerging or unconventional methods for computation stretches every mind in the classroom—including the teacher's! Class ended with the homework assignment: a short set of multiplication problems to be illustrated with drawings of base-10 blocks and with arithmetic. Some students asked if they could use the "backwards" method for the latter; Kerri

| FIGURE 5.3 | Megan's "Backwards" Method of Multiplication for $2 \times 18$ |
| --- | --- |

- Multiply 2 x 1 and write down the product, 2, under the 1.
- Multiply 2 x 8 = 16. Write the 6 in 16 under the 8 and 2.
- Write the 1 in 16 above the 1 in 18.
- Add the 1 to the 26, arriving at the correct product, 36.

$$
\begin{array}{r}
1 \\
18 \\
\times\ \ 2 \\
\hline
26 \\
+\ 1 \\
\hline
36
\end{array}
$$

agreed and chose to start the lesson the next day by pushing on student understanding of place value.

## Discourse and Problem Solving

We've all seen the same rules of thumb for solving mathematics problems: Make a model or diagram. Make a table, chart, or list. Guess and check. Consider a simpler case. Look for patterns. In classrooms in which rich discourse is encouraged, these methods surface within the context of daily lessons. When students solve problems by whatever method makes sense to them and share their work, many strategies can arise within the context of one problem. Take, for example, the pizza problem alluded to in Chapter 3 (Lappan, 1998):

> A large pizza was stored in the cafeteria refrigerator for five nights. During the first night a pizza thief took half of the pizza. The second night the thief took half of what was left. Each night the culprit stole half of the remaining pizza. How much of the pizza was left after the fifth night? If the pizza were left in the refrigerator for a long time, how many nights would pass before the pizza was completely gone? (p. 46)

Students may use several different strategies to solve this problem. Some might make a diagram of the pizza, sectioning off the parts eaten each night; others may use arithmetic, creating a simple table showing the amount of pizza left after each night; still others may set up a coordinate grid and plot values in order to look for patterns and make predictions. Students who are confused need to consider a simpler case involving only one or two nights before being able to work toward the final solution.

Rich, deep, and argumentative discussions occur when students display their work and present their strategies. As students explain their thinking, others can see connections and the usefulness of different methods. It is our responsibility as effective teachers to watch the flow of the lesson so that students not only solve the problem, but also learn about the strengths and weaknesses of different strategies. Summarizing and labeling the strategies makes them memorable, as does naming them in honor of the students who came up with them (e.g., Mary's Method, Theo's Theory, Pedro's Plan).

## Discourse and Vocabulary

As one teacher said to me, "It's vocabulary, vocabulary, vocabulary." For him, the key to students' understanding was familiarity with mathematical words and their meanings. But the traditional approach of handing students a list of words and asking them to look up their definitions doesn't work. Students don't really know what definitions mean until they've grappled with the concepts to which the words are applied. What a great opportunity to encourage discourse! Understanding develops as students use and hear words in context (Bullock, 1994). I suggest that we use classroom discourse to develop the concepts before introducing mathematically specific terms. As the NCTM (2000) notes, "It is important to avoid a premature rush to impose formal mathematical language; students need to develop an appreciation of the need for precise definitions and for the communicative power of conventional mathematical terms by first communicating in their own words" (p. 63).

Teachers need to be very attentive as they encourage students to use standard vocabulary when they talk and write. We need to really listen in order to uncover misunderstandings; students are apt to parrot back definitions, thus concealing their confusion. During lessons in which students first encounter a new concept, teachers should encourage them to describe ideas in their own words before introducing the specialized terms.

In one 5th grade classroom I observed, the teacher wanted students to grapple with the ideas of perimeter and area without introducing the terms themselves. She began by having the students trace their feet on grid paper. They explored ways to figure out how many squares were within the traced region and how many linear units were in the string they had glued around the tracing. As students shared ideas, they spoke about the number of squares inside the "footprints" and the number of units along the foot's "ring" or "rim." Students continued to use these terms as they developed the concepts of perimeter and area. Over the next few lessons, the teacher frequently used the terms "area" and "perimeter" herself, leading her 5th graders to definitions and a natural use of the terms.

## Using Concept Maps to Foster Discourse

When my 7th graders were working on a unit about circles and investigating the relationships between radius, diameter, circumference, and area, I used a modified version of Frayer's concept map to help them (1969). Many but not all of my students had become comfortable with the estimation that the circumference of any circle is about three of the diameters and that the area is about three times the radius squared; a few had started using 3.14 (or $\pi$) instead of 3 as the value in their formulas. I gave them blank copies of the concept map and had them write "circumference" in the central portion.

Each student worked individually to fill in the sections labeled Definition, Facts, Examples, and Nonexamples. Figure 5.4 shows responses from two of the students.

After students had completed their maps, I asked them to show their partners what they had written. This type of pair-share is an effective way to help students sort out misconceptions and practice clear explanations prior to a full class discussion.

As the partners shared their models with the whole class, I recorded their ideas on a large sheet of chart paper. The first definition came from Lou: "Circumference is the distance around a circle." I asked for more definitions and recorded several, including Annekki's: "The path that makes the circle." The class decided that Lou's definition was easy to say and understand but confusing because it sounded as though he was referring to the space outside the circle rather than the line. Gradually, consensus evolved around Annekki's definition.

We moved on to the "Facts" section of the concept map. I started the discussion by requesting statements that did not use any formulas. Even though I wanted students to understand the circumference and area formulas, it has

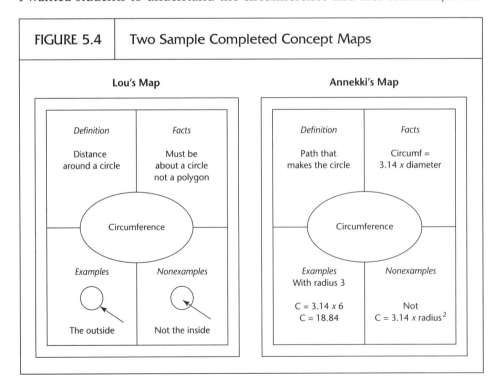

| FIGURE 5.4 | Two Sample Completed Concept Maps |

been my experience that the more general ideas get pushed aside once a discussion of formulas begins. Lou's comment that "circumference must be about a circle, not a polygon" was eye-opening for some. Other students talked about the investigations they'd done with string, reminding classmates that they needed a bit more than three "diameter strings" to cover the circle's circumference. Examples and nonexamples popped up as the students talked, and the discussion segued easily into summarization of ideas about the formulas. The richness of this lesson was in the discourse. Using the concept map without the sharing would have helped students record their own ideas, but would not have expanded their thinking.

Murray (2004) suggests using concept maps in a way that incorporates a significant amount of discourse. Her students created concept maps to be featured in parent-student-teacher portfolio conferences at the end of a trimester. Each student created a concept map for a big idea from the semester's work on operations and was required to follow a clear set of guidelines. After teacher conferencing and editing, Murray "divided the class into groups of three so that the students could practice their presentations, each student in turn making an oral presentation while the remaining two played the roles of parents. . . . We could not have found a better way to practice using the language of mathematics in a meaningful way. During the actual conferences, students made confident presentations and parents expressed appreciation for having learned about mathematical relationships they had previously never really understood" (p. 75).

## Summary

As we change our teaching, it is important to realize that we expect students to change with us; they also have new responsibilities. The quick-reference table in Figure 5.5 summarizes teacher and student roles in classroom discourse as described by the NCTM (1991).

Students may well be uncomfortable shifting from passive observers to active learners. How can we help them learn these new skills? In some cases, it may help to explicitly explain that the class will operate in a new way; in others, it may be better to let the students' new roles develop gradually, as the teacher comes to be seen more as an inquirer.

Regardless of how you make this transition, research shows that students learn better when they are actively involved in discussing and arguing about

| FIGURE 5.5 | Teacher and Student Roles in Classroom Discourse |
| --- | --- |

| Teacher's Role | Student's Role |
| --- | --- |
| Poses questions and tasks that elicit, engage, and challenge each student's thinking. | Listen to, respond to, and question the teacher and one another. |
| Listens carefully to students' ideas. | Use a variety of tools to reason, make connections, solve problems, and communicate. |
| Asks students to clarify and justify their ideas orally and in writing. | Initiate problems and questions. |
| Decides which of the ideas students bring up to pursue in depth. | Make conjectures and present problems. |
| Decides when and how to attach math notation or language to students' ideas. | Explore examples and counterexamples to investigate conjectures. |
| Decides when to provide information, when to clarify an issue, when to model, when to lead, and when to let different students struggle with a problem. | Try to convince themselves and one another of the validity of particular representations, solutions, conjectures, and answers. |
| Monitors student participation in discussions and decides when and how to encourage each student to participate. | Rely on mathematical evidence and argument to determine validity. |

*Source:* Adapted from information in *Professional Standards for Teaching Mathematics,* by the National Council of Teachers of Mathematics, 1991, Reston, VA: Author.

ideas. As teachers, it is our mission to get them involved, and classroom discourse does it! Classrooms become exciting learning spaces when teachers establish a culture of shared ideas and guide students as they discuss their mathematical understanding. And when students thrive, teachers experience the exhilaration of making it happen.

# 6

# Creating Mathematical Metis

*Joan M. Kenney*

The Greek word metis is not often heard in current conversation, yet it captures a strong sense of the capabilities and competencies that are a major goal of current mathematics education. David Brooks (2000) describes *metis* as a faculty that the French might equate with *savoir-faire* or the Germans with *gestalt*. The Yale anthropologist James Scott (1998) talks about metis in the context of a toolbox of knowledge and practical skills that enables people to respond to change.

One of the primary attributes of metis is that it cannot be taught or memorized; it can only be imparted and acquired. Brooks provides the example of the apprentice who may exhaustively learn the rules of cooking but who will not have the same awareness as a master chef in regard to when the rules or recipe should be applied and when they should be adjusted. Similarly, a beginning teacher may studiously digest a book on pedagogy, but only a metis-rich teacher will be able to successfully guide students as they struggle to achieve understanding of complex content. Skillful arithmetic students may perform superbly as human calculators, but they will always be surpassed by the metis-endowed mathematics students who have a "feel" for the connections and underlying concepts involved in the problem at hand.

I have found that people in metis-rich environments tend to converse rather than lecture. They develop a sense of the processes and relationships in the world around them, and comprehend the complex patterns of learning. Having metis means being aware of the flow of ideas; it means knowing which thoughts can go together, and which will never connect. It means knowing how to react when the unexpected occurs, and how to tell what is really important from that which is mere distraction. Metis is not scientific knowledge, but rather a special sensitivity to one's particular circumstances.

People who prize metis welcome a diversity of approaches; people who acquire it tend to learn by doing, rather than solely by abstract reasoning.

In a series of professional development workshops designed around the theme of creating and cultivating mathematical metis, I asked participants to produce a list of attributes that they saw as contributing to a general sense of metis. Their lists included such traits as openness, curiosity, resourcefulness, persistence, risk-taking, intuitiveness, and awareness. Participants felt strongly that if these features are operative in a mathematics classroom, the potential for true mathematical metis exists, as evidenced by the seeing and making of connections and the ability to generalize to conclusions.

The strategies and examples offered in this book all focus on how to create a sense of comfort with mathematical objects and actions. When this connectedness is reinforced, while at the same time the distinction between content and process is kept clear, students are able to move beyond blind memorization and black-box algorithms. They become skilled at

- Selectively reading mathematics text,
- Writing with clarity about their mathematics thinking,
- Using a wide range of graphic representations to explore and explain their mathematics comprehension, and
- Discussing their strategies with other students.

## Creating Metis for Teachers and Administrators

As important as it is to create metis for students, it is equally vital for teachers and administrators to achieve a sense of intuitive mathematical understanding. They need to collect information on the following issues:

- How does mathematics learning takes place?
- What are the important mathematics concepts—the "big ideas"?
- What benchmarks can be used to evaluate mathematics teaching?
- What are the effects of high-stakes testing on metis in general, and on mathematics learning in particular?

Current brain research provides us with many insights into how we first learn mathematics. New technologies produce a physical mapping of brain activity that enables us to describe, with far greater precision and sophistication than ever before, how learning takes place. Researchers such as Lawrence Lowery (1998) give us new ways to think about what level of mathematics is developmentally appropriate to teach at certain grades. For example, at what point is the human brain ready to make the transition from a two-dimensional to a three-dimensional mapping of space? Obviously, such questions have significant implications for when certain mathematics concepts should enter the curriculum. Equally obviously, if mathematics concepts are introduced too early, students will suffer an immediate loss of metis. Grade-level expectations have been definitively set out in the NCTM standards, and are mirrored to varying degrees by state and district standards. But elementary and middle school teachers are confronted with a great deal of new curriculum that has "trickled down" from the upper grades, particularly in the areas of geometry and data and statistics, and these new topics are competing for precious instructional time with an increased emphasis on testing. Therefore, in order to preserve any sense of metis for both students and teachers, it becomes vital that the *truly* important and developmentally appropriate mathematics concepts be clearly identified at each grade level, and that the mathematics be taught through a series of connections rather than as isolated lessons.

In their role as instructional leaders, administrators need to have a rigorous, intuitive understanding of mathematics concepts. The expansion of their mathematical comfort zone will enable them to validate benchmarks and guide programs to successful conclusions; their metis will help them to have an instinct for when to hold the course, and when it is prudent to change direction.

It is critical that educators document the effect of accountability measures and high-stakes tests on mathematics learning. Holding all students to high expectations and agreed-upon standards is a positive goal, but many of the methods used to assess progress are destructive. If our goal is to give students an awareness of connections and a sense of comfort with the mathematical world, the process will not be enhanced by curriculum that is devoted to preparing them to answer multiple-choice or single-fact questions. This is the antithesis of metis.

# Action Research as an Aid to Metis

Translating education research into practice is a complex and multi-layered process. A study by Hemsley-Brown and Sharp (2003) suggests that action research can stimulate involvement by educators, and that the transfer of research to practice requires strong relationships between researchers and practitioners. Because the coauthors and researchers of this book *are* practitioners, the story of how the book came about serves to illustrate the merging of research and practice, and how this merging promotes metis.

I had been asked to provide professional development for four senior coaches from the Massachusetts Mathematics Coaching Program, funded by the Noyce Foundation. My goal was to design a professional development experience that went beyond the usual model of a scripted workshop. I had recently read two books that I found engaging: Barton and Heidema's *Teaching Reading in Mathematics* (2000), which led me to think about producing a guidebook specifically for the mathematics classroom that would extend the investigation of literacy beyond the topic of reading; and Michael Grady's *Qualitative and Action Research* (1998), a practitioner's guide to designing research projects, collecting and analyzing data, and reporting research results.

Setting the talented senior coaches to the task of investigating the connections between reading, writing, and other forms of communication in the mathematics classroom promised to be an enriching, metis-building endeavor. Practitioners, no matter how experienced, do not tend to see themselves as researchers or writers; they do not have ready access to many research journals, and are often intimidated by the jargon that clogs so much educational writing. However, if they are provided with a scaffolded, structured environment in which to assess the research, they can quickly become empowered and stimulated to transfer the research to their classroom practice, resulting in the creation of a strong climate of metis for both teacher and student.

In the Appendix to this book you will find agendas for the professional development sessions that provided the structured environment in which this book was created. Through observing how they are designed and becoming familiar with the readings, teachers and administrators will hopefully be stimulated to learn more about the language of mathematics, to incorporate this knowledge into practice, and to create a metis-rich environment for mathematics teaching and learning.

## Task Clusters

Teachers and administrators can only achieve metis if they have a firm grounding in the important mathematics concepts, and an idea of how these concepts develop across grade levels. To facilitate this process I have found it useful, as a professional development practice, to create collections of "cluster tasks"—groups of four or five mathematics tasks that share a common content topic, such as area and perimeter, estimation, or inverse operations (Kenney, 1999). Each cluster includes a problem from primary, elementary, middle, and high school grades, and the following set of focus questions is provided for participants to discuss:

- What is the *core mathematics* that these tasks have in common?
- What additional mathematics concepts or skills are involved?
- Are there concepts or skills that are unique to certain tasks?
- For what grade level or levels does each task seem most appropriate?

Working the tasks and discussing the focus questions, both in small- and large-group settings, provides a unique opportunity to probe for connections and have a substantive dialogue about mathematics content. It is interesting that, at first glance, teachers often feel that certain tasks are too difficult for the grade level for which they were designed. However, it often turns out that it is the reading level, not the mathematics, that is perceived as being too difficult. The strategies for improving the reading of mathematics text provided in this book can alleviate this situation.

These task clusters were originally designed to give elementary teachers a sense of how the fundamental mathematics concepts they teach will emerge and develop over the ensuing grades; however, the strategy has proved to be equally effective for use in professional development with middle and high school teachers. Because this group rarely has either the opportunity or the inclination to think about what a basic concept might look like at the kindergarten or elementary level, the exercise of solving and discussing the cluster of tasks becomes most illuminating. Not only does the point at which concepts are refined and extended become clear, but the discussions across grade level provide important clues about the misconceptions that occur in the early years and that can lead to relentless confusion in the upper grades. For example, is the fact that students in 9th or 10th grade are so often unable to clearly and mindfully articulate the difference between area and perimeter due to a lack of understanding that occurs at a certain point in mathematical learning, or is it something that is inexplicably engrained from the first time the two concepts are encountered? Or, why do older students immediately rush to use an algorithm to solve a problem, but are so often unable to decide which formula to use?

## What Students Need to Know

Some interesting information has emerged from the Mathematical Association of America's (MAA) revision of its recommendations for the undergraduate program in mathematics. The MAA Committee on the Undergraduate Program in Mathematics (CUPM) is primarily concerned with mathematics instruction in the first two years of college, and with what incoming students need to bring with them from their secondary mathematics experience. At the MAA's annual meeting in 2001, CUPM hosted 13 focus groups involving a total of over 180 mathematicians; the informal reports of each of these groups reveals some strong recurring themes. Here are a few of the characteristics that focus group attendees want to see in their students:

• A comfort, or metis, with symbols and graphs and an ability to use graphs as a language. Mathematics professors want students who can both create new graphs from given information and analyze provided graphs as descriptors of mathematical activity. It is thus essential that students be exposed to graphs beginning in the early grades.

• A deep conceptual understanding of their mathematical studies, particularly in regard to functions. One professor rather plaintively wrote that he wished students would "listen to the equations." Certainly, an ability to be truly "tuned in" to what mathematics symbols are saying is a high form of metis.

• The ability to speak the language of spreadsheets. Creating spreadsheets is a comprehensive mathematical activity; it requires students to fully integrate their modeling, transforming, inferring, and communicating skills. What a splendid activity to use for assessing mathematical proficiency!

• The ability to show multiple representations of a mathematical problem. One positive outgrowth of the NCTM standards and the use of constructed-response assessments is that young students are being encouraged to visualize the mathematical world in a variety of ways, through programs such as "Read It, Draw It, Solve It" (Miller, 2001). With minimal adaptation, these resources can be used to lead learners to read the initial problem, to draw a picture of what the text is saying, and to represent their solution pictorially, numerically, and verbally. If this becomes a consistent method of problem solving in elementary school, students develop habits of mind that will stand them in good stead as they move on to the more complex mathematics of middle school, high school, and college.

If students can write clearly about mathematics in both words and in symbols, provide graphic representations (either as diagrams or as graphs), and articulately justify their strategies and how their solutions connect with those of their classmates, then they have certainly developed a deep, rich understanding of the underlying concept.

# Final Thoughts

This book contains a wealth of strategies and suggestions for improving students' ability to read mathematics text, to write about their mathematical thinking, and to enhance their communication through graphic representation and discourse. Some of these suggestions will resonate with you and match your teaching style; others may seem cumbersome or time-consuming. To improve your own skills, consider trying one of the strategies that you are *not* naturally drawn to. It is only in this way that you can experience firsthand the discomfort, the cognitive dissonance, and the disruption of metis that a task presented in a certain format, or with a certain unique vocabulary, may produce in a student. It is only through this type of experience that we become sensitive and responsive to *all* our students, not just to those who see the mathematical world through the same lens that we do.

# Appendix

# Structured Agendas
# Used to Research This Book

*Note:* Full citations for all readings listed in this appendix can be found in the References and Resources section.

## Session 1

- Goals for the project.
- Descriptions of mathematical literacy.
- Reflection on how each participant acquired a second language (open discussion).
- Discussion of common threads in language acquisition.
- Beginning list of mathematics vocabulary.
- Working with visual representations
    - That stimulate vocabulary development.
    - That inform text.

**Assignment:** Create a concept map for "percent" and a Frayer model for "prime."

**Reading:** "Using Graphic Organizers to Improve the Reading of Mathematics" (Braselton & Decker, 1994)

## Session 2

- Presentation of concept maps and Frayer models.
- Reflection on how each participant acquired mathematical language (open discussion).
- Discussion of "Teaching the Language of Mathematics" (Krussel, 1998).
- Refining of graphic organizers for specialized use in mathematics.

**Assignment:** Write a comparison of personal experience in acquiring a second language, and in acquiring mathematical language.

**Readings:**
• *Semantic Aspects of Quantity* (Schwartz, 1996)
• *Assessing Mathematical Skills and Understanding Effectively* (Schwartz & Kenney, 1999)
• "Handwriting Mastery" (Allen, 2003)
• *Text Organization and Its Relation to Reading Comprehension* (Dickinson, Simmons, & Kameenui, 2000)

## Session 3

• Sharing of language acquisition comparisons.
• Sharing of reading assignments from last meeting.
• Introduction to *Reading and Writing in Mathematics,* 2nd ed. (Barton & Heidema, 2002).
• Introduction to action research and *Qualitative & Action Research* (Grady, 1998).
• Exploration of various bibliographies using a library research catalogue.
• Document search at university library.

**Assignment:** Write up a draft focus paper.

**Readings:**
• "Strategies to Support the Learning of the Language of Mathematics" (Rubenstein, 1996)
• "Mathematics as a Language" (Usiskin, 1996)
• "Using Student Contributions and Multiple Representations to Develop Mathematical Language" (Herbel-Eisenmann, 2002)

## Session 4

Language work update and overview:
• Question: "Why is it so difficult?"
• Discussion of personal experiences of language impeding mathematical learning.
• Discussion of content development and literacy issues using sample tasks from *Balanced Mathematics Assessment for the 21st Century* (Schwartz, 2000).

- Discussion of focus questions:
    - What difficulties does each task represent in the areas of vocabulary, format, reading level, lack of clarity, and ambiguousness?
    - What changes would you make to the text in order to facilitate access to the mathematics?

## Session 5

Continuation of literature review:
- "The Role of Reading Instruction in Mathematics" (Curry, 2004)
- "Teaching Content Area Vocabulary" (Graves, 2004)
- "Literacy in the Language of Mathematics" (Bullock, 1994)

**Assignment:** Write up an incident around mathematical language that you observe in a classroom, or interview a teacher regarding language issues.

**Readings:** The following articles are all from the November 2002 issue of *Educational Leadership:*
- "From Efficient Decoders to Strategic Read" (Vacca)
- "Teaching Reading in Mathemathics and Science" (Barton, Heidema, & Jordan)
- "Advanced Math? Write!" (Brandenbury)
- "Seven Literacy Strategies That Work" (Fisher, Frey, & Williams)

## Session 6

- Sharing of draft chapter summaries.
- Continuation of literature review:
    - *What Mathematical Knowledge Is Needed for Teaching Mathematics?* (Ball, 2003)
    - "Language Pitfalls and Pathways to Mathematics" (Barnett-Clarke & Ramirez, 2004)
    - "The Role of Reading Instruction in Mathematics" (Curry, 2004)
    - "Math Lingo vs. Plain English: Double Entendre" (Hersh, 1997)

## Session 7

Discussion of questions raised at Boston Higher Education Conference on High School Literacy, April 2003:
- What does it mean to be literate in different content areas?
- What do we mean when we say that students can't read?

• What do students need to do to read for meaning in a content class-room?

• What is the content teacher's responsibility for teaching students to use reading as a learning tool?

**Readings:**

• *Writing to Learn Mathematics: Strategies That Work, K–12* (Countryman, 1992)

• *Writing in Math Class: A Resource Guide for Grades 2–8* (Burns, 2002)

## Session 8

Report on progress of writing, difficulties, and changes in direction.

**Reading:** "Reporting Research Results" (Grady, 1998, pp. 35–42)

# References and Resources

*Note:* Included in the following bibliography are full citations for all works explicitly cited within the body and appendix of this book, as well as additional resources that we found valuable and significant in our research.

Albert, L. R. (2000). Out-in—inside-out: 7th grade students' mathematical thought processes. *Educational Studies in Mathematics, 41*(2), 109–141.

Albert, L. R., & Antos, J. (2000). Daily journals connect mathematics to real life. *Mathematics Teaching in the Middle School, 5*(8), 526–531.

Allen, J. (2003). *Yellow brick roads: Shared and guided paths to independent reading.* Portland, ME: Stenhouse Publishers.

Allen, R. (2003, Summer). Handwriting mastery: Fluent form is crucial for expression. *ASCD Update.*

Anderson, N. C. (2002, November). *Student explanations of mathematical reasoning.* Paper presented at the National Council of Teachers of Mathematics Eastern Regional Conference, Boston, Massachusetts.

Armstrong, T. (2003). *The multiple intelligences of reading and writing.* Alexandria, VA: Association for Supervision and Curriculum Development.

Aspinwall, L., & Aspinwall, J. (2000). Investigating mathematical thinking using open writing prompts. *Mathematics Teaching in the Middle School, 8*(7), 350–353.

Association of Teachers of Mathematics in Maine. (2000, Winter). I have, who has? *ATOMIM Newsletter, 11.*

Baldwin, R., Ford, J., Smith, C. (1981). Teaching word connotations: An alternative strategy. *Reading World, 21,* 103–108.

Ball, D. L. (2003). *What mathematical knowledge is needed for teaching mathematics?* Remarks prepared for Secretary's Summit on Mathematics, U.S. Department of Education.

Barnett-Clarke, C., & Ramirez, A. (2004). Language pitfalls and pathways to mathematics. In R. Rubenstein (Ed.), *Perspectives on the teaching of mathematics*. Reston, VA: National Council of Teachers of Mathematics.

Barton, M. L., & Heidema, C. (2000). *Teaching reading in mathematics*. Aurora, CO: Mid-Continent Research for Education and Learning.

Barton, M. L., & Heidema, C. (2002). *Teaching reading in mathematics* (2nd ed.). Aurora, CO: Mid-Continent Research for Education and Learning.

Barton, M. L., Heidema, C., & Jordan, D. (2002, November). Teaching reading in mathematics and science. *Educational Leadership, 60*(3), 24–28.

Baxter, J., Woodward, J., Olson, D., & Robyns, J. (2002). Blueprint for writing in middle school mathematics. *Mathematics Teaching in the Middle School, 8*(1), 52–56.

Behrmann, M. M. (1995). Assistive technology for students with mild disabilities. (ERIC Digest E529)

Berger, A. (1989). Ways of activating prior knowledge for content area reading. In D. Lapp, J. Flood, & N. Farnan (Eds.), *Content area reading and learning: Instructional strategies* (pp. 118–121). Edgewood Cliffs, NJ: Prentice-Hall.

Borasi, R., Siegel, M., Fonzi, J., & Smith, C. (1998). Using transactional reading strategies to support sense-making and discussion in mathematics classrooms. *Journal for Research in Mathematics Education, 29*(3), 275–305.

Brandenbury, M. L. (2002, November). Advanced math? Write! *Educational Leadership, 60*(3), 67–68.

Branford, J. D., Brown, A., & Cocking, R., (Eds.). (2000). *How people learn: Brain, mind, experience, and school*. Washington, DC: National Research Council.

Braselton, S., & Decker, B. (1994). Using graphic organizers to improve the reading of mathematics. *The Reading Teacher, 48*(3), 276–281.

Brooks, D. (2000). *Bobos in paradise*. New York: Simon & Schuster.

Bullock, J. O. (1994, October). Literacy in the language of mathematics. *The American Mathematical Monthly, 101*(8), 735–743.

Burns, M. (2002). *Writing in math class: A resource guide for Grades 2–8*. Sausalito, CA: Math Solutions Publications.

California State University Writing Center. (2003). *Helping ESL students improve their writing*. Los Angeles, CA: Author.

Carroll, J. A. (1991). Drawing into meaning: A powerful writing tool. *English Journal, 80*(6), 34–38.

Chamot, A., & O'Malley, J. (1994). *The CALLA handbook: How to implement the Cognitive Academic Language Learning Approach*. Reading, MA: Addison-Wesley.

Clement, L. (2004). A model for understanding, using, and connecting representations. *Teaching Children Mathematics, 11*(5), 97–102.

Countryman, J. (1992). *Writing to learn mathematics: Strategies that work, K–12*. Portsmouth, NH: Heineman.

Curry, J. (2004). The role of reading instruction in mathematics. In D. Lapp, J. Flood, & N. Farnan (Eds.), *Content area reading and learning* (2nd ed., pp. 227–241). Mahwah, NJ: Lawrence Erlbaum.

Dehaene, S. (1998). *The number sense: How the mind creates mathematics.* New York: Oxford University Press.

Devlin, K. (2000). *The math gene.* New York: Basic Books.

Dickinson, S., Simmons, D., & Kameenui, E. (2000). *Text organization and its relation to reading comprehension.* Eugene, OR: University of Oregon Press.

Draper, R. J. (2002). School mathematics reform, constructivism, and literacy. *Journal of Adult and Adolescent Literacy, 45*(6), 520–529.

Education Development Corporation. (2001). *The use of speech recognition by students and in schools: An overview.* Available online: http://www.edc.org/sph2wrt.

Educational Performance Systems. (2001). *LINKS secondary resource handbook.* Woburn, MA: Author.

Fay, L. (1965). Reading study skills: Math and science. In J. Figural (Ed.), *Reading and inquiry* (pp. 93–94). Newark, DE: International Reading Association.

Fisher, D., Frey, N., & Williams, D. (2002). Seven literacy strategies that work. *Educational Leadership, 60*(3), 70–73.

Frayer, D. A., Frederick, W. C., & Klausmeier, H. G. (1969). *A schema for testing the level of concept mastery.* Working paper No. 16. Madison, WI: University of Wisconsin.

Gardner, H. (1983). *Frames of mind.* New York: Basic Books.

Goldsby, D. S., & Cozza, B. (2002). Writing samples to understand mathematical thinking. *Mathematics Teaching in the Middle School, 7*(9), 517–520.

Grady, M. P. (1998). *Qualitative and action research.* Bloomington, IN: Phi Delta Kappa Educational Foundation.

Graves, M. (2004). Teaching content area vocabulary. In D. Lapp, J. Flood, N. Farnan (Eds.), *Content area reading and learning: Instructional strategies* (pp. 218–224). Mahwah, NJ: Lawrence Erlbaum.

Hemsley-Brown, J., & Sharp, C. (2003). *The use of research to improve professional practice.* Summarized in *ASCD ResearchBrief, 2*(22), 1–3.

Herbel-Eisenmann, B. A. (2002). Using student contributions and multiple representations to develop mathematical language. *Mathematics teaching in the middle school, 8*(2), 100–105.

Hersh, R. (1997). Math lingo vs. plain English: Double entendre. *The American Mathematical Monthly, 104*(1), 48–51.

Jubinville, L. (2002). *Guide for writing response in mathematics.* Unpublished manuscript.

Kenney, J. M. (1999). *Cluster tasks across the Balanced Assessment curriculum.* Cambridge, MA: Harvard Graduate School of Education.

Kenney, J. M. (2002). Basic skills and conceptual understanding: It's not either/or. *ENC Focus, 9*(3), 26–28.

Krussel, L. (1998). Teaching the language of mathematics. *The Mathematics Teacher, 91*(5), 436–441.

Lamour, N. (2003). *Should ESL students learn to write in English?* Cambridge, MA: Lesley College.

Lapp, D., Flood, J., & Farnan, N. (Eds.) (1989). *Content area reading and learning: Instructional strategies.* Englewood, NJ: Prentice-Hall.

Lappan, G., et al. (1998). *Connected mathematics: Bits and pieces II.* Saddle River, NJ: Prentice Hall.

Lappan, G., et al. (2002). *Connected mathematics: Accentuate the negative* (p. 148). Upper Saddle River, NJ: Prentice Hall.

Lappan, G., et al. (2002). *Getting to know connected mathematics: An implementation guide.* Upper Saddle River, NJ: Prentice Hall.

Lappan, G., et al. (2004). *Connected mathematics: Variables and patterns* (p. 24). Upper Saddle River, NJ: Prentice Hall.

Lappan, G., et al. (2004). *Connected Mathematics: How likely is it?* (p. 24). Upper Saddle River, NJ: Prentice Hall.

Lesh, R., Post, T., Behr, M. (1987). Representations and translations among representations in mathematics learning and problem solving. In C. Janvier (Ed.), *Problems of representation in the teaching and learning of mathematics* (pp. 33–41). Hillsdale, NJ: Lawrence Erlbaum Associates.

Lowery, L. F. (1998). *The biological basis of thinking and learning.* Berkeley, CA: FOSS Program, University of California.

Maloch, B. (2002). Scaffolding student talk: One teacher's role in literature discussion groups. *Reading Research Quarterly, 37*(1), 94–112.

Martinez, J., & Martinez, N. (2001). *Reading and writing to learn mathematics: A guide and resource book.* Boston, MA: Allyn Bacon.

Marzano, R. J., Pickering, D. J., & Pollock, J. E. (2001). *Classroom instruction that works: Research-based studies for increasing student achievement.* Alexandria, VA: Association for Supervision and Curriculum Development.

Massachusetts Department of Education (2002). *Release of Spring 2002 MCAS Test Items.* Malden, MA: Author.

Mathematical Association of America (2001). *Mathematics and the mathematical sciences in 2010: What should students know?* CUPM preliminary report. New Orleans, LA: Author.

McConnell, J., et al. (1990). *University of Chicago School Mathematics Project: Algebra.* Glenview, IL: Scott Foresman.

Michigan State University (1998, Spring). *Technology-enhanced learning environment web (TELE-Web).* Available online: http://tele.educ.msu.edu.

Miller, E. (2001). *Read it, draw it, solve it: Grades 1–5.* Lebanon, IL: Pearson Learning Group.

Murray, M. (2004). *Teaching mathematics vocabulary in content.* Portsmouth, NH: Heinemann Publishers.

National Council of Teachers of Mathematics (1991). *Professional standards for teaching mathematics.* Reston, VA: Author.

National Council of Teachers of Mathematics (1996). *Communicating in mathematics, K–12 and beyond.* Reston, VA: Author.

National Council of Teachers of Mathematics (2000). *Principles and standards for school mathematics.* Reston, VA: Author.

Perlin, M. (2002). Rewrite to improve. *Mathematics Teaching in the Middle School, 8*(3), 134–137.

Phillips, J. (1979). The problem with math may be reading. *Instructor, 89*(4), 67–69.

Pimm, D. (1987). *Speaking mathematically: Communication in mathematics classrooms.* London: Routledge.

Pisauro, J. A. (2002). I catch the pattern! *ENC Focus, 9*(4), 18–23.

Polya, G. (1973). *How to solve it: A new aspect of mathematical method.* Princeton, NJ: Princeton University Press.

Pugalee, D. K. (2002). Beyond numbers: Communicating in math class. *ENC Focus, 9*(2), 29–32.

Readence, J. W., Bean, T. W., & Baldwin, S. (1998). *Content area literacy: An integrated approach* (6th ed.). Dubuque, IA: Kendall Hunt Publishing Company.

Reehm, S. P., & Long, S. A. (1996). Reading in the mathematics classroom. *Middle School Journal, 27*(5), 35–41.

Reinhart, S. C. (2000). Never say anything a kid can say. *Mathematics Teaching in the Middle School, 5*(8), 478–483.

Riordan, J., & Noyce, P. (2001). The impact of two standards-based math curricula. *Journal of Research in Mathematics Education, 32*(4), 368–398.

Robinson, J. (2000). *The missing link: Essential concepts for middle school math teachers.* Burlington, VT: Annenberg/CPB.

Rubinstein, R. (1996). Strategies to support the learning of the language of mathematics. In P. Elliot (Ed.), *NCTM Yearbook* (pp. 214–219). Reston, VA: National Council of Teachers of Mathematics.

Schneider, J., & Saunders, K. (1980). Pictorial languages in problem solving. In S. Krulik (Ed.), *Problem solving in school mathematics: NCTM yearbook* (pp. 61–69). Reston, VA: National Council of Teachers of Mathematics.

Schoenfeld, A. H. (1987). What's all the fuss about metacognition? *Cognitive science and mathematics education.* Hillsdale, NJ: Lawrence Erlbaum Associates.

Schwartz, J. L. (1996). *Semantic aspects of quantity.* Unpublished monograph.

Schwartz, J. L., et al. (2000). *Balanced mathematics assessment for the 21st century.* Cambridge, MA: Harvard Graduate School of Education.

Schwartz, J. L., & Kenney, J. M. (1995). *Assessing mathematical understanding and skills effectively.* Interim report of the Balanced Assessment Program, Harvard Graduate School of Education, Cambridge, Massachusetts.

Schwartzman, S. (1994). *The words of mathematics: An etymological dictionary of mathematical terms used in English.* Washington, DC: Mathematical Association of America.

Scott, J. (1998). *How certain schemes to improve the human condition have failed.* New Haven, CT: Yale University Press.

Spanos, G. (1993). *ESL math and science for high school students.* Paper presented at the 3rd National Research Symposium on Limited English Proficient Student Issues. Washington, DC: National Clearinghouse for English Language Acquisition.

Stanish, B. (1999). *The ambidextrous mind book.* Carthage, IL: Good Apple Press.

Stigler, J. W., & Hiebert, J. (1999). *The teaching gap.* New York: The Free Press.

Sullivan, K. (1982). Vocabulary instruction in mathematics: Do the "little" words count? *American Reading Forum Yearbook, Vol. 2,* 9–11.

Swindal, D. (2000). Learning geometry and a new language. *Teaching Children Mathematics.* Reston, VA: National Council of Teachers of Mathematics.

Thompson, D., & Rubinstein, R. (2000). Learning mathematics vocabulary: Potential pitfalls and instructional strategies. *Mathematics Teacher, 93*(10), 568–573.

Usiskin, Z. (1996). Mathematics as a language. In P. Elliott (Ed.), *NCTM 1996 Yearbook* (pp. 231–243). Reston, VA: National Council of Teachers of Mathematics.

Vacca, R. (2002). From efficient decoders to strategic readers. *Educational Leadership, 60*(3), 6–11.

Warren, A. (2002). *MATHPLAN: A diagnostic and prescriptive collection for the elementary grades.* White Plains, MD: Author.

Woleck, K. (2001). Talking their way to the middle of all numbers. *ENC Focus, 8*(3), 29–31.

Wylde, H. C., & Partridge, E. H. (Eds.) (1963). *Complete and unabridged Webster dictionary, international edition.* New York: Little and Ives.

Zinsser, W. (1989). *Writing to learn.* New York: Harper & Row.

# Index

Note: Information presented in figures is denoted by *f*.

# About the Authors

**Joan M. Kenney**'s professional career has encompassed a wide variety of experiences in the field of mathematics. She has worked as a research scientist, specializing in operations analysis and risk management; taught mathematics at the secondary and college levels; and performed task modeling and pedagogical intervention in elementary and middle school classrooms. Joan served as the national evaluator for the National Science Foundation's Assessment Community of Teachers and Connecting with Mathematics projects, the Council for Basic Education's Instructional Leadership Academy, and the Digi-Block program. She has delivered keynote addresses at several national and international conferences, and has written extensively about mathematics education reform and assessment.

Joan recently retired from the Harvard Graduate School of Education, where for 10 years she was the Project Coordinator and Codirector of the Balanced Assessment Program. During that time she was involved in assessment task design, student performance evaluation, and outreach to community stakeholders; she also served on the Mathematics Task Force of the Massachusetts Board of Higher Education, and on the original design committee for the Massachusetts Comprehensive Assessment System. She continues to consult with school districts on issues of mathematics curriculum and classroom practice, and to provide professional development for teachers and administrators in the areas of mathematics content and assessment. Joan may be contacted by e-mail at joan_kenney@post.harvard.edu.

**Euthecia Hancewicz** is a mathematics teacher coach, trainer, and consultant currently working with middle and elementary schools. She has taught mathematics from grades 2 through 10, focusing mainly on middle school students.

As a participant in the Noyce Foundation's Massachusetts Mathematics Coaching Project, Euthecia witnessed firsthand how teachers worked to change their practice in light of current research. During those years, she began to write about the power of classroom discourse—a valued part of her personal teaching style.

Euthecia earned a Bachelor of Arts in Psychology at Westhampton College, University of Richmond, Virginia, and a Masters of Education from the University of Massachusetts at Amherst. She is an active member of the National Council of Teachers of Mathematics (NCTM), the National Council of Supervisors of Mathematics, and the National Staff Development Council, and has been a presenter at the NCTM national conference. She continues the coaching and facilitating work to further her conviction: "The best way to help young people learn to think is to help them learn mathematics." Euthecia may be reached at e.hancewicz@comcast.net.

**Loretta Heuer** is a Senior Research Associate at Education Development Center's (EDC) K–12 Mathematics Curriculum Center in Newton, Massachusetts. A former elementary school teacher, Loretta has worked as a middle school mathematics coach and as an implementation advisor in urban and suburban districts through the Massachusetts Mathematics Coaching Project. She has trained elementary school principals in mathematics using EDC's Lenses on Learning program, and is currently coaching a team in EDC's Lesson Study Communities project. Loretta's main research interests are the use of interactive technology in professional development and the role of graphic representation in the learning of mathematics. She can be reached at lorettamath@yahoo.com.

**Diana Metsisto** started her career as a programmer and systems analyst working on scientific, real-time systems. After 11 years she switched to education, where she worked as a 7th grade mathematics teacher for 23 years in Norwell, Massachusetts. She then served as a mathematics coach for three years under the auspices of the Massachusetts Middle School Mathematics Project. For the past two years, Diana has been a consultant for the Education Development Center, working as a coach with teams of middle and high school mathematics teachers for the Lesson Study Communities Project.

Diana received a Bachelor of Arts in Mathematics from Northeastern University and a Master of Arts in Critical and Creative Thinking from the University of Massachusetts. She is interested in finding ways for students and teachers to develop mathematical understanding and power and in researching how we think about and solve problems and develop conceptual understanding. Diana believes that this is best accomplished by listening, dialoguing, and reflecting on learning experiences. She may be reached at dianamets@comcast.net.

**Cynthia L. Tuttle** taught mathematics for 21 years at both the elementary and middle school levels and worked as a certified reading teacher. She served as an Assistant Professor at both Castleton State College and American International College, where she was the first Coordinator of Supportive Services for Undergraduates with Learning Disabilities. She has been a mathematics coach in middle school classrooms for the Massachusetts Mathematics Coaching Project, and has worked with teachers through the Hampshire Educational Collaborative. At present, she works independently as a mathematics coach and consultant.

Cynthia earned her Doctorate of Education at the University of Massachusetts. Throughout her career, she has concentrated on strategies to help all students, including those with learning disabilities, succeed in mathematics. She believes strongly that every student has a right to achieve his or her full potential in mathematics and that every teacher has a responsibility to assist in accomplishing this goal. Cynthia may be reached at cyndituttle@yahoo.com.

# Related ASCD Resources
# Literacy Strategies for Improving Mathematics Instruction

At the time of publication, the following ASCD resources were available; for the most up-to-date information about ASCD resources, go to www.ascd.org. ASCD stock numbers are noted in parentheses.

## Audio

*Improving Mathematics Instruction Through Coaching* by Glenda Copeland (#505298)

*Reading Strategies for the Math Classroom* by Rachel Billmeyer (#205063)

*Three Steps to Math and Reading Success* by Lauren Armour (#202202)

## Books

*The Beginning Schools Mathematics Project* by Anne McKinnon and Don Miller (#195264)

*Math Wonders to Inspire Teachers and Learners* by Alfred S. Posamentier (#103010)

## Video

*The Brain and Mathematics, Tape 1: Making Number Sense* (1 tape and facilitator's guide, #400238)

*The Lesson Collection: Math Strategies, Tapes 17–24* (8 tapes, #401044)

For more information, visit us on the World Wide Web (http://www.ascd.org), send an e-mail message to member@ascd.org, call the ASCD Service Center (1-800-933-ASCD or 703-578-9600, then press 2), send a fax to 703-575-5400, or write to Information Services, ASCD, 1703 N. Beauregard St., Alexandria, VA 22311-1714 USA.